ACKNOWLEGMENTS

I would not have completed this memoir without the sustained encouragement of Betsy and John whose opinion was of paramount importance for me to continue writing.

Special thanks to Lorri who often helped with spelling especially before I discovered the computer's spell self check.

All this would not be possible without the kind and generous help and guidance of Diana Poirier, our lovely friend and neighbor. She so often got me out of the depths confusion and frustrations because I was so computer challenged.

To dear Mishenka,
such a good friend
and a wonderful
human. With love
George

Larchmont 6/16/06.

PROLOGUE

With apologies to Nabokov I shall plagiarize the title of his memoirs "Speak Memory", to head mine, as it fits my needs and not because of any literary pretensions on my part. Also as this monograph is not intended for a formal publication, I hope that my audacity may be forgiven. I often thought that I might want to recall my earlier life, especially so since the birth of my grand children. They experienced so little of the 20th Century, while I contrast have lived over seventy years in it. Having been borne between the two world wars and having survived the Holocaust of the German occupation of Eastern Europe, I consider myself having lived a borrowed life. Much has been written, recalled by individuals or espoused by various media about the horrors of those years. I thought that perhaps Ned, Zoë, Mathew and Aaron, as they get older, might be interested to know that their Grandfather lived through it all. That he was one of few who lived driven by a blinding will to survive, wanting to tell of the cataclysmic injustice, but not less also, by a desire for vengeance and even a sense of adventure. Nevertheless, if the truth be told, such survivals should be attributed to blind luck and little to one's initiative. I will try to recall these events to the best of my memory. Some will I remember from occasional retelling, other are acutely fresh in my mind, and then there are the occasional, unexpected sudden flash backs to a long forgotten crises.

As I start to write and think about my past, one memory begets another. They tumble out of my head, yet my memory for names is, as it always was, very poor. I would fudge on those occasions by substituting the forgotten name with one which might fit the situation by the virtue of the nationality, ethnic background or a social status.

TABLE OF CONTENTS

THE EARLY YEARS

Home and Childhood

I will begin then by describing my childhood and attempt to give some sense of time and place of the life in a small provincial town in Eastern Europe in the first half of the 20th.Century. I will then go over the war years. There are countless historical books describing the events leading to the German invasion of Poland and the beginning of the Catastrophe of World War II. I will focus therefore, not on the historical but on the personal drama as my life evolved, between September 1939 and May of 1945, years that hang heavy on my mind. Times which in a large measure were marked by an intense isolation, daily humiliation, need, insecurity and fear. Yet in the end, it catapulted me to a great adventure and gave me a sense of purpose and hope. These musings are particularly poignant because of the contrast between then and now, as I begin to write this memoir, sitting on our patio in the idyllic surroundings of a verdant garden, surrounded by flowers, the bird songs and the rhythms of the tidal river, in mid July of the millennium year 2000

I was born in the southwestern Polish town of Katowice, in the province of Silesia on June 16, 1926. The circumstances were somewhat unusual since I was born in a hospital rather than in the house, as was the custom at that time. In fact my mother traveled there, to avoid being delivered in our hometown because of the recent death of her friend, in childbirth. This woman died as the result of Puerperal Fever, which in the pre-antibiotic days was the scourge of childbearing. The choice of Katowice was mandated by the more advanced medical facilities of a large city and a readily available family support consisting of my grandmother and my mother's two sisters.

The little town of Radomsko where we lived was situated on then the western border of Poland mid way between its two pivotal cities: Krakow the ancient, and Warsaw the current capital of the country. Just a few miles south of us was a larger city named Czenstochowa. It was a town of great religious and national significance because of the country wide annual pilgrimage to worship the Black Madonna, at Jasna Gora, an impressive fort like monastery

on a hill. The object of the worship was a rather dark small icon-like painting, of the Virgin Mary holding baby Jesus. Its historical significance was based on the belief that it was through the intervention of the Holy Mother in response to the prayers and pleading of the local population, that the then invading Swedish army was stopped and defeated in Czestochowa at the gates of Jasna Gora. That victory marked the end of the Swedish aggression against Poland in the latter part of the 17th Century. This half legend became so embedded in the national and religious psyche of Catholic Poland, that in spite of the rather drab attributes of Czenstochowa and indirectly the neighboring Radomsko, by the virtue of its proximity to it, was well known beyond its borders.

Radomsko of my childhood was not especially an attractive little town and even less so fifty years later when Edith and I came to visit there. This was still in the days of Communist government and its attendant paranoia. (I was taken to the local jail by five Policemen and interrogated for a few hours because I took photographs of local train station and the factory associated with my father's history). Radomsko was primarily an industrial town that depended on its large and varied furniture manufacturer, as well as, a major steel industry. There were several large furniture factories. One in particular was a branch of a well known Austrian firm of Thonet Mundus which was producing bent wood chairs, commonly found in restaurants and cafes, through out the world. (Some years ago, when skiing in Aspen I saw such chairs in a café there. Having recognized at once their unique shape, I won a bet when I proclaimed with conviction that not only these were made in Poland, but probably in my old town.) One of the other major furniture factories was owned by the family, Wunsche, who were even in the days of the thirties, rich enough to summer in Monte Carlo and winter in Switzerland. (A prominent scion of this originally German family was a life long friend of uncle Ludwik's and will be mentioned later, because of his heroic behavior in saving a number of Jews during the war.) As well as, the large industrial furniture complex, there were also dozens of outstanding individual carpentry and cabinet workshops owned by very skilled artisans who hand crafted high quality furniture for national consumption and world wide export. As I recall it, this furniture was mostly done in a style resembling the Viennese Biedermeiyer period. It was all handcrafted with such basic tools, as the saw, the plane and the hammer. I liked visiting these workshops, having had an easy access to them, as my

father's business was supplying them, as well as, the local factories, with such essential hardware, as screws and nails. As a child I was quite fascinated to watch them creating from coarse plain wooden planks elaborate pieces of furniture. These would then be surfaced at first with dull sheets of veneer, which when finally stained, polished and varnished, would highlight the beautiful patterns of its surface. This process was not without some discomfort, as it usually took place in very small, cramped workshops, filled with an intense odor of fresh varnish or nauseating stench of hot animal glue, which left me with strong olfactory memories to this day. The presence of the furniture industry spawned a number of sawmills on the periphery of our town. As children, we delighted to wallow in the tall mounds of sawdust smelling of pine or watch the large tree trunks being converted to long heavy wooden planks by the giant saws of the mill. The noise of the saw and the sparks like sawdust whirling all round was especially exciting. The other dominant industry was the manufacture of such steel products as wire, nails, screws and in the late thirties, even armaments. The preeminent factory by the name of Metalurgia, employed some two thousand men in a town of thirty thousand inhabitants. It was my understanding that it was the largest factory of its kind in the country. It featured prominently in our lives because my father represented it and was responsible for selling its products throughout central Poland. Metalurgia was part of a large French steel and armaments industrial complex of Schneider - Creseaux. In Radomsko its director was a Frenchman, Mr.Rafaelli, who to a child like myself, loomed like a princely figure. He lived in a very elegant villa and was one of the few who owned a car, a Citroen, I believe. That was in the days when there was only a single hand operated gas pump in town.

Radomsko was shared between Christians and Jews. The latter was a relatively large community, representing about a third of the total population. There was a tendency for the two groups to live in separate clusters, but there was no Ghetto per se. There was generally little social intermixing, if there was any, it usually took place among the more affluent and educated members of both groups.

Looking back on Radomsko, stripped of the mist of nostalgia, I recall it to be quite a miserable little town, with out real attributes. It offered little in term of culture or music; it

even lacked the essential creature comforts. Learning French, playing the piano or the violin however, was possible under private tutelage. Of your two great uncles, Ludwik played the violin, Bob the piano, while I started learning French. None of us however, accomplished these tasks, with any distinction. Though we had a grand piano in our living room, I remember little music being played in our home, unless it came from the radio. There was an adequate Public Library.

Our home was located in the center of the town, only a few houses from its main square. We lived in a relatively large apartment within a housing complex of fourteen other units rented out by my father, to other tenants. Our family lived in that part of the building that faced the street. It contained besides our flat on the first floor, a large space on the ground level devoted to my father's business for storage and the distribution of the merchandize. Also on the ground floor, separated by a drive-in gated passage, was a tavern. The gate was large enough when fully opened to allow a truck to enter, when closed it had on one side a small door, for daily use. Called "brama" in Polish; it was similar to the gates which can still be seen to this day, in some older parts of European cities. The other, a much larger building was at a right angle to ours, facing a rather long narrow cobbled stoned courtyard, at the end of which was a small garden. Each May the lilac bloomed around the time of my parents wedding anniversary, anchoring a happy memory. I also vaguely recall attempting to growing vegetables there, but with uneven results. What I remember well, however, is the public latrine at the very end of the building, the only lavatory facility available for the tenants come rain or shine. Needles to say it was highly odiferous. Yet, in contrast, the apartments were quite spacious, usually well furnished by their middle class tenants. I think there was only cold running water available in the kitchens, and there were no bathrooms. Just in case there was no adequate water pressure, there was a large circular hand pump in the yard, making a loud clanking noise when turned manually, which required serious effort. The presence of the tavern in our building, provided some occasional excitement, often unwelcome, caused by drunken brawls or other unseemly incidents, due to the legendary Polish affinity for vodka. Overall, I have considered the presence of the tavern or "knaipa" as it was called in Polish, in the midst of our daily life, exciting and rewarding. In particular, I was fond of the type of food served there, which to this day I seek whenever I can.

Fortunately, now New York abounds in traditional Polish restaurants where such dishes as tripe, pork cutlets and blintzes are prepared the old way. Veal hot dogs, a great variety of Polish hams and sausage are also now available in New York. One memory, which stayed with me all this time, was that of watching the tavern's kitchen maid sitting on the door steps, crying her eyes out, while grating the fresh horse radish root for a condiment. This must be the most lachrymose of all the root vegetables, causing intense watering of the eyes, far worse than while cutting onions.

Our apartment, which was relatively large, served both as my father's office and as our home. The office always held a special interest for me as it offered play space outside the working hours and during inclement weather. There were several desks with typewriters. What really held my interest there, was a massive iron copying press, with a turn screw topped by a wooden turn handle. This rather primitive press, not far removed from those of Gutenberg's time, was then the current way of coping letters or the business documents. The typed letters or hand written notes written in a special India ink were the placed against moisten sheets of tissue-like paper were put in to the press By turning the screw, a solid iron plate slowly descended to put these papers under great pressure, so as to make a permanent copy. When the copies dried, they were then placed in a folder for permanent record or future reference. I was always eager to participate in this process not only to be of help but because I was intrigued how the copies would come out or if they were even be readable at all.

The rest of the apartment consisted of my parents' bedroom with a balcony facing the street. In the winter, the balcony served as a convenient storage place for Vodka, which on one occasion almost proved my undoing, when I took a swig without realizing that it was from a bottle of a 100% proof spirit. Then there was an ample room furnished with carved dark oak Victorian pieces and a grand piano. It served both as a dining room and as the parlor. There were several large windows, which during a fierce thunderstorm would rattle alarmingly, while the flashes of lightning seemed close by. There was a door leading to the children's room, which for the last six years before the war, I shared with Bob. The kitchen was a rather primitive affair with an old-fashioned coal fired stove on one side and storing cupboards on the other. The wash sink with cold water only, was at the window facing the courtyard.

Besides the daily cooking chores, the kitchen was used for two other essential functions: laundry and bathing. The baths were taken in a tin tub the size and shape not unlike the one, in which Marat is portrayed at his death. The water was heated in large pots on the kitchen stove.

This cumbersome effort might perhaps explain why public baths remained a necessity in the Eastern Europe until very late, while a few still exist even in New York to this day. Here however, their popularity is ascribed to other, than their hygienic utility. There were some homes in Radomsko, which even then, had all the modern comforts. While we had cold running water and a lavatory with a water closet, we lacked a proper bathroom with a tub. The presence of the only functional indoor lavatory in the whole complex made us very popular with friends and neighbors, who would grace us with a frequent visit. I however, was always a little suspect of they motivation. The family washing was also done in the kitchen, in a large wooden tub, resembling a wide half barrel. It rested on three stools and had a hand-operated wringer on its edge. The personal washing was hang out side to dry and then smoothed with an iron heated repeatedly on the stove. The art was to get the bottom of the iron heated well enough to press, but not to burn the cloth, which required frequent spitting on the forefinger to test the heat. The bed sheets and table cloths were taken by our maid Bella, to a hand operated "mangle" a few door away. This was a mysterious contraption consisting of very long, very smooth, somehow heated wooden rolling pins, which would iron the bed linens smooth. These sheets while still warm, now smelling fresh, were folded into a manageable size for storage. I am probably right in thinking that such domestic short comings were also likely to be found in the poorer parts of American large cities or in some rural areas of the country, in those times The other seasonal kitchen chores in which I loved to participate were the preparations of different preserves for winter. The most elaborate ritual was reserved for pickling the cabbage for Sauerkraut. Bushels of it would be brought by a farmer in a horse driven wagon each fall, to be shredded, then put into a barrel with lots of coarse salt and caraway seeds. The barrels were then taken down in to the coal cellar where then they were covered with a linen cloth, followed by a loose wooden top, which was weighted down with a heavy stone. After weeks of fermentation, it was then uncovered with great anticipation to be eaten either raw or used in hot meals, throughout the long winter and

spring. Fresh vegetables were not available, as they are today through the year, so the pickled cabbage was a great source of Vitamin C in the winter months. Oranges, lemons and an occasional banana were available, but were expensive, so were considered a luxury for special treats.

Other fun chores that I particularly like to assist with was making Cranberry perseveres and Raspberry jams. These were cooked in large copper pots with copious amounts of sugar. Incidentally, these copper pots, made by the wandering Gypsies, were of very high quality and considered family heirlooms by most households. The telephone at that time was a large wooden contraption with a mounted mouthpiece and a hand held round receiver connected by a thick wire which when not in use, hung in a metal cradle. There was a small crank, which had to be rapidly turned in a clockwise direction to request the required number verbally from the local exchange. The radio by the time I became a teenager however, was quite a sophisticated reliable instrument, with a choice of wavelengths and an oscillating electronic eye, reflecting the quality of reception. American comics were available in translation, but the ones I liked best were those by Disney, which were printed in very vivid colors on a glossy paper. National newspapers were available daily.

There were some other places of interest to a young boy, such as a very elaborate, comprehensive stationary store, which was a must to visit throughout the school year ,but especially so, after each vacation to replenish one's satchel with pens, pencils and papers. There was a particular brightness about the store because of items of many colors .It smelled of fresh printer's ink and had an infinite variety of arts and crafts materials. Not that I had any talent for painting or drawing but browsing there was always fun. Another store that held great fascination for me was a rather well stoked luxury food "emporium", which announced its sophistication by dead rabbits, pheasants and other assorted wild game birds in their splendid feathers, hung by their feet on its outside doors. French sardines, Bordeaux wines and all kind of delicatessen were available. I made sure that I accompanied my father, when he went there to buy gifts for his clients or business associates or for the occasional treats for the home. Not far from that store was a very fine café and patisserie, which was most probably more than subliminal inducement for me to tag along with my father, as invariably

we would stop there. Another activity that was fun for me was to await for him at the railroad station, especially on the return from a long business trip. On our way home, I would sit grandly along his side in a horse driven "doroszka". If he happened to return from Torun, a town in the northwestern Poland, famous for its chocolate covered gingerbread cookies, which were my favorite, I was sure to get some. One year when I was spending my summers at a sleep way camp, he sent me a large box of these, which I shared s with my friends. I was very popular for a while. In my early teens I liked to help in the business activities along with my mother, who was deeply involved in the management and was of great support to father. I liked especially the sorting and packing of the smaller items such as screws packed in cardboard boxes. Occasionally I would even stack the heavy wooden cases of nails one upon another, in a brick like fashion, from floor to ceiling. I was often entrusted to carry cash, checks or promissory notes (weksle) to the bank. These are probably no longer used as means of delayed payment now, as they were then. In Poland, before the war it was a very common and it extensively utilized by business people, especially when short of immediate cash. The blank note was issued; I think by some official entity. It resembled a check and had watermarks so it could not be falsified. The debtor would then write in the appropriate amount signing personally the promissory note, for payment for a latter date.

The sum owed would consist the original amount owned, with an additional percentage proportional to how far long the actual payment was delayed. When occasionally such payments were not met, the debtor could be sued. Another method to cash the "weksel" was ahead of its maturity, when it could be discounted for a broker's for fee. At times, I would be asked to go to the post office to send or receive telegrams, send money orders or was entrusted to make bank deposits. Although my participation may not have been very necessary, it was never the less appreciated by my father and perhaps even a source of pride for him, as well as, for me.

There were number of childhood pleasures such as going to the neighboring confectionary for a creampuff sprinkled generously with powdered sugar. Among my other favorite treats, especially on a hot summer's day, was getting a glass of a well chilled club soda topped and sweetened with raspberry syrup. I felt however, always a little miffed, as it was a tad less

sweet than I liked. The soda jerk would only dispense enough syrup to make it pink .These days I drink it ruby red, as I can buy the syrup for it in the Polish or Russian stores in Queens with the greatest of ease.

There was only one cinema in town, named without much imagination Kinema; K in Polish sounds like a hard C in English. The generic name for a cinema was Kino, thus a direct transposition from English to Polish, of cinema. It is no great surprise that a trip there was a greatly anticipated pleasure and even a sense of adventure. It was a virtual exposure for me to the world beyond our little town. Cowboys and Indians, slapstick comedies such as Abbott and Costello or Harold Lloyd hanging on to the clock, were my favorites. I have a particularly strong memory of the film "War of the Worlds" based on the book by H.G. Wells. In the earlier years of my childhood, I was usually taken by my brother Bob who was then called by the name of Noldek, a diminutive of Arnold. He considered this a chore, as he would take me much to his chagrin, only upon the urging of our mother. He would much rather go to the cinema with friends of his own age. I was after all a full five years younger than he was. Sometimes, to show his resentment, he would walk so fast, that I had a hard time keeping up. When I reached the age of ten, I was finally allowed to go there with friends or by myself. I must add that going to the cinema was allowed very liberally, as it offered not only entertainment, but also a program of World news among other features. Nowadays, television makes it irrelevant, but back then such a visual exposure was a world outside. Even immediately after the war, when I was in London, there were still cinemas dedicated entirely to presenting only World and National news in a weekly format.

Among other hallmarks of Radomsko worth mentioning, was the local "Apteka" or pharmacy. Then, it was entirely dedicated to medicines and sanitary products, unlike the current drug stores like CVS. At that time, there were hardly any over the counter drugs available, other than aspirin. All medical prescriptions had to be individually dispensed according to the doctor's order and had to be mixed by hand. It might be worth mentioning that the 20th.Century was known also as the "Aspirin Age". The availability of over the counter drugs began with Aspirin, which has created a therapeutic revolution, by allowing for self-medication. It is worth noting, that this simple drug known by its generic name as

salicylic acid was found useful for myriads of therapeutic uses, other than just the relief of pain, even to this day. The interior of the "apteka" was a rather cool and cavernous space, with the walls lined by mahogany cabinets containing glass or porcelain jars of various sizes, with labels in Latin. The atmosphere of sterility and chemical odors enveloped one immediately on entry. Whenever I was sent there with a prescription or to collect the medicines ordered, I would feel not exactly a fear, but had at least some anxiety. The apothecary was a man of aloof dignity. During the war, he apparently exhibited great courage, having helped a number of people at the risk of his own life. The pharmacy was situated just outside the Ghetto, thus he was apparently able to support and even rescue some Jews. The paradox was, that before the war he was known to be a leading member of "Endeks", an extreme nationalist party, with strong Anti-Semitic leanings.

The Family

Through out my childhood, I used to spend my winter vacations with my mother's family in Katowice, a large industrial town that was in a center of a coalmining district in the Polish part of Silesia. As you might recall, I was born there. I enjoyed these vacations on several levels. I liked being surrounded by the welcome warmth of an extended family, which consisted of my Grandmother, two aunts and their children. I was especially close with my older cousin Ludwik Jakubowicz. The highlight of the visit was the unusual opportunity to see every film in town for free, as Ludwik's father worked for the local branch of the Paramount Film Studios. He had access to unlimited free passes to any and all cinemas there. I liked the big town atmosphere of Katowice, especially in the early evening hours with the hustle and bustle of the pre Christmas crowds on the snow-covered streets. The many stores were illuminated by multicolored neon signs, which added to the excitement. There even was a branch of Woolworth's on the main street, a commercial outpost of the then, far distant America. I vividly recall inhaling second-hand cigar smoke on an overcrowded, steamy tramcar while enjoying the ride. It seemed so sophisticated to me, when contrasted with the best of what Radomsko had to offer for transportation which was one horse drawn "doroszka". In the best Austro-German tradition, there were several fine cafés, to which my mother would take me when meeting her friends. On such visits to the cafés, hot chocolate

with cream puffs on the side, were de rigueur. Even when I would roam the town by myself, I would stop for a dollop of the wonderfully tasting “Schlagsanne”, a heavy whipped cream with a touch of vanilla and sugar. The other tasty morsel was the proverbial hot dog, sold steaming hot by the street vendors. My Grandmother was very suspicious that I ate some whenever I lacked an appetite for dinner and she was right.

Among my family, I liked my aunt Helena best. She was mother’s youngest sister. I stayed either with her in Katowice or with my other aunt Zosia, also a very nice person. Helena was a dentist, who was married to a near-do-well doctor, but a well educated, cultured, and an interesting man. They had a little girl rather late in life, which I adored. When I reflect on the tragedy of the Holocaust, it is the murder of such innocent little children which is most poignant and unforgivable.

My parents were such a significant part of my childhood. I will try to describe them and their background in detail. My father Leopold came from a modest family, who nevertheless, even in those early times of emancipation, had some university-educated relatives. I believe that my father’s education probably stopped after high school. One of his brothers, Uncle Herman was a complicated man, a dentist, a wealthy real estate owner and as every one said, a miser. Ludwik recalls that during the early days of the war when they were both in Vilno, the Russian occupied part of Poland, he helped Uncle Herman recover a very substantial hoard of gold and other valuables. When soon after, Ludwik asked him for a relatively modest amount of money which he desperately needed for a ticket for the Trans-Siberian train to Vladivostok, Herman pleaded poverty. Yet having survived the war, rescued with the help of Catholic nuns, first from the Russians then from the Germans, he had enough wealth to donate all his estate to the Church. So much so, that at his funeral he was mourned by the church as the sainted benefactor Franczizek (Francis, was his latter assumed first name). I did however keep in contact with his only remaining son Richard, a dentist in Grenoble, France, whose daughter and son, both visited with us in the past. Recently, we had the pleasure of meeting with Nelly and her husband Gilbert, in Marseille. In fact, their daughter Karen spent eight months in New York, in a doctoral program in jurisprudence at Columbia, where we saw her frequently. When Edith and I visited Richard and his wife Marie in

Grenoble in 1957 on our way from South Africa to Canada, they were most hospitable. We had a memorable trip to Chamonix with them.

Of my father's sister and four other brothers, I only knew Uncle Max who lived next to us in Radomsko. Another brother Felix died rather early. His wife Ruzia had a pension in Kamisko,our summer retreat. We met with her and her very lovely daughter Stella, a few years my senior, in Lublin in the early days of the war. They too vanished without a trace. My uncle Max and his very formidable wife, also named Ruzia, had two children. Their daughter Irka (Irene) was a very close childhood companion, whom I recall very fondly and you will see her mentioned again.. She survived the war under an assumed name and now lives in Israel and Sweden. She in turn had a son Kobe and a daughter Erelka, whom we met on several occasions. Kobe had an interesting career in pioneering the work on dental implants in Sweden where he now lives. He is now a senior executive in an international Pharmaceutical firm. Uncle Max however, was the bane of my father's existence. He had a hard time supporting his family, having to rely heavily on my father's support, which occasionally lead to predictable family squabbles. I have only a vague recollection of my father's parents, as they were already quite old and sick when I was a very young child.

Before World War I, my father earned a living as a commercial traveler, but one with great panache. He traveled the length and width of the Great Russian Empire. His journeys took him from Archangels on the North Sea to the Crimea on the Black Sea and from Moscow in the West to Vladivostok in the far reaches of the East Asia. He would recall fondly a leisurely vacation sailing on the great river Volga. Occasionally, he would regale us with tales of his various adventures. Beside Polish, he spoke Yiddish, fluent in Russian and German, which included some smattering of poetry and songs. He also traveled to the eastern part of Germany and Austria. Vienna, in particular at that time, was considered the Paris of Eastern Europe. I recall his enthusiasm describing the painting by Raphael, known as the Blue Madonna, which he saw while visiting a museum in Dresden, Germany. In his bachelor days, he summered occasionally in Switzerland. I remember a photo of him standing on the edge of a lake in a one peace black swimsuit, seemingly ready to dive into the water. In a way, he was a man of many parts. He was also a man of short temper, which is so

characteristic of most of the Kleiners. Yet he had a great sense of humor, loved practical jokes but disparaged pretensions. He was generous, participating responsibly in the civic and social life of the town, where he was well respected.

For as long I can remember, my father was involved in only one business, which was representing Metalurgia, a large steel factory producing primarily, wire, nails and screws. It was located in Radomsko, employing about two thousand workers at that time. It was part of a large French conglomerate. My father had the sole distribution rights for the whole of central Poland, then a land of thirty million people. I have described some of it elsewhere, so I will only mention in addition, that it required frequent and extensive travel.

He and my mother were married on May 10, 1917, in the pen-ultimate year of World War I. It is interesting note how different were the conditions for the civil population, particularly for the Jews in Radomsko then, as compared to World War II. Such events as weddings and planning for future were most unrealistic in the confines of the Ghetto. In contrast the German occupation during the first World War was relatively benign except for serious shortages of food. There were however, no serious restrictions of personal freedoms and other civil rights.

My Mother came from the neighboring town of Czestochowa, which was briefly described earlier, in this chapter. She came from a relatively emancipated family with many siblings. Her eldest brother Pavel (Paul) was an officer in the Polish Legion under Marshal Pilsudski. He participated in the liberation struggle for Polish independence after 150 years of occupation by Russia, Germany and Austria. By that time, he married a Catholic, having converted earlier to Catholicism himself. When in 1920 there were some severe anti-Semitic excesses in Czestohowa, bordering on pogrom where some Jews were beaten up or had their beards forcibly cut, by the marauding soldiers lead by a General Haller, Uncle Pawel mustered the local garrison under his command. He not only managed to put stop to it, but also chased the whole mob out of town. Pavel eventually left with his family for Mexico, where he was appointed the Polish consul. I was very proud to have his old saber on the wall in our house, with which I played war games with my friends. Fortunately, no injuries

resulted from this horseplay. He was however a source of great disappointment for me. When he came to our house, for the final fair wells, I have extracted a promise from him, that as soon as he gets to Mexico, he was to send me a pair of cowboy boots with spears and a sombrero. I must have been no older then six or seven at the time, yet I am still waiting to this day.

Before I can continue with the saga of my uncle Pavel, I must digress here to tell, about a most unexpected and exiting incident, which involved my Brother Ludwik many years later. Ludwik, managed to escape from Soviet Russia, against all odds. Not only did he lack adequate funds for a ticket on the Trans-Siberian train from Moscow to Vladivostok, but also he left without the all important, essential Japanese transit visa, for his final destination to Canada. On arrival to Vladivostok, after a journey of six thousand miles across the vastness of Russia, he went to the Japanese consulate, to be told, that its function there was for commercial purposes only. He approached the local consular officer with a plea that if such visa will not be granted, then the only sure outcome will be Ludwik's banishment to the Siberian Gulags or worse. The Japanese Consul relented, despite the governmental edict, with the proviso, that Ludwik sends a telegram to the remaining friends in Vilno, that under no circumstances can any one leave, without obtaining a visa first, as such will not be granted in Vladivostok again, under any circumstances.

Ludwik and his friend Julek Tigner remained in Japan for several months where they were treated very well. While in Mocow Ludwik traded some of his clothing for money, buying with it Russian Postage Stamps. There was very little postal communication at that time between the Soviet Union and the rest of the world. As the Russian stamps were rarities Ludwik by selling them, was able to have enough money to live well for the rest of their stay in Japan. He and a group of others in similar circumstances, left for Canada just before the attack on Pearl Harbor. There, he and his friends have joined the Polish army in exile. They were among the many volunteers from the North and South Americas.

Soon after arrival to Canada in their newly minted Polish Army uniforms, they were parading in front of a group of various dignitaries, when Ludwik whispered to his friend Julek Tigner

"you will not believe me, but do you see this tall colonel there among the other officers, that is my uncle Pavel" and indeed it was. They were both given an immediate furlough, which they spent in New York City. Most of the volunteers were promptly transferred to England to fight the war, but Ludwik remained in Canada for some time. I must add, however, that my Brother Ludwik's career in the army, could be best described as ranging somewhere between the adventures of the "Good Soldier Schweik "and Sergeant Bilko. My brother Bob, on the other hand was a truly heroic "Mosquito Pilot in the Polish Air force under British Command. Uncle Pavel and his family eventually settled in Cuba after the war, where I think they lived under difficult circumstances. I heard a rumor that he divorced his first wife and married a Cuban. I have a telephone number in Havana for a Ludwik Garbinski , which I am certain must have been Uncle Pavels eldest son, but I had hard time contacting him.

My mother's brothers, Zygmunt and Henry, both lived in Warsaw. I visited Zygmunt and his family several times before the war. He was married to a very pretty woman with whom he had daughter, who was much younger than I. Visiting with them was very special treat for me, as being in Warsaw, the Capital city, was always a great adventure. They lived in an elegant apartment and were most hospitable at all times. Warsaw before the war was a very vibrant city. It was a tragedy and disgrace how the Germans early in the war and then later during the Polish National Army uprising, destroyed this great city beyond recognition. When the Red Army was at the gates of Warsaw, there was a popular uprising against the German occupiers. The Polish freedom fighters were hoping to establish local political and administrative control allied to the Government in exile in London. In any other situation, this would have been a rational move if the Russians were liberators, not occupiers. They had their own Polish Government in exile, which was diametrically opposed to the one in London. It was composed of a hard core Polish Communists, who spent the war years in Russia. On Stalin's directive, the Soviet Army stopped their unstoppable advance to sit and wait across the river Vistula that divided the city in two. They set and waited until the Germans reduced the city to rubble and sent hundred of thousands of the defeated freedom fighters, both men and women, into concentration camps. This the second such perfidious incident by Soviet Russia, although this time indirectly, conspiring with the Nazi Germany against the Polish Nation while the world watched.

Uncle Zygmunt and his family also ended tragically. At the beginning of the war he became somehow, separated from them. For a short while, he was together with Ludwik in Vilno. He returned to Warshaw to rejoin his wife and child, where they all vanished with the elimination of the Warsaw Ghetto. We have lost contact with them early in the war, as the postal communications internally between the different Ghettos in Poland were virtually non-existent. Paradoxically the Germans did allow some foreign mail delivery. Ludwik sent us some very welcomed care packages before he left Vilno and later from Japan. It is difficult to describe what joy such gift parcels bought us at that time.

My mother's younger brother Henry, an architect, also lived in Warsaw, but I have only fragmentary memory of him. We did however, hear rumors that he was somehow a member of the Jewish police hierarchy, or was in charge of a factory in the Ghetto working for the Germans. This news did not endear him to us. We lost contact with him already early in the war.

My two remaining aunts (the youngest Helen was mentioned before) could not be more divergent, with regard to both their personality and physical appearance. Where Zosia was petite and very nice, Aunt Erna in contrast, was a heavyset woman with a personality to match. She also happed to be my Godmother, an assignment that she did not fulfill with alacrity, over my childhood years, much to my disappointment. On her infrequent visit from Belgium she would never bring me a present, nor pay any special attention to me at all. The family lore had it, that she was responsible for almost sending me to an early grave as infant, when she scratched my arm with her finger nail, which then apparently resulted in a life threatening infection. Echo of the wicked witch? She, her husband and their three sons lived in Brussels before the war. Erna and her two younger sons survived, but she has lost her husband and their oldest son Ludwik in an extermination camp. Somehow we resumed the contact with each after the war. Edith and I visited them on our way form South Africa to Canada, a trip that incidentally turned in to a very special experience. It was not because of a particularly warm welcome, which was pleasant enough, but because we had an opportunity in 1957 to travel there on a helicopter. To this day, I pat myself on the back for having the

gumption to it. Edith was such a sport to join me in this adventure. One can imagined how exciting, such a trip was for us then. We rose perpendicularly from a center of Paris, over its rooftops, with a wonderful view of the city below. The helicopter with the windows opened, flew then low over the Loire valley, on a sunny July afternoon. Landing in the middle of Brussels just behind the Grand Place, we feared that any second, we might be impelled by the tall spires of the nearby Cathedral. It is difficult to do justice in describing the drama of such a landing. I am certain that these days they have a heliport in a less congested part of the city. But what fun it was in retrospect. We have kept in touch with Cousin George, who even visited me in New York.

Aunt Zosia, who lived in Katowice in a spacious apartment on pleasant square, was most hospitable whenever we visited them. Her son Ludwik spent a short time with us in the early days of the Ghetto and I alluded to him else where in this memoir. He too vanished without a trace, as did his parents and his sister.

My Grandfather Ludwik Garbinski died before I was born, but My Grandmother was a significant presence in my early childhood, of which I have fond memories. During the war, on our return to Radomsko from the east, she lived with us in our cottage in the Ghetto. I was glad in a way that she died before the Ghetto was eliminated, so she at least avoided the indignities of the transport in a cattle car and the horrors the camps, which would have resulted any way, in an inevitable death.

My mother Tola, a diminutive of Teofila, was a very gracious, calm person with charm and modest dignity. She had no university education, but did attend a finishing school and was quite proficient in French. My Father relied heavily on her wisdom and advice. She was of enormous help in running the family business, especially during my father's absence, on his frequent travels. She was not much involved in running the house as we always had domestic help. Mother was well respected and liked by our community. As I was significantly younger than my brothers were, I was her baby and companion, especially in my Father's absence. I would often tag along to visit her friends for tea or lunch. Although I must say, when there were no other children in the house, on such visits, I would be bored. I loved to accompany

Mother to town for the occasional chores at the various artisans, such as the shoemaker or a tailor or to buy a bale of cloth for a garment. I was quite fascinated by the process of choosing a material, which would eventually be turned into a suit, a gown or a coat. The dilemma to determine, how much exactly, was needed, for each specific garment, was a judgment call shared between the buyer and the seller. Once measured, cut and wrapped, it was taken to the dressmaker or the tailor. At that time ready-made clothing was not easily available, so getting a new suit would require a very careful set of measurements by the tailor, choice of patterns and several subsequent visits refit at each stage of completion. When the garment was finally finished by hand, it was then tried on, with great anticipation in front of a mirror. Nowadays, only the very wealthy can afford bespoke clothing or hand made shoes. A visit to a shoemaker was of particular interest for me. I liked watching him take an imprint of a sole of a shoe, then with small, simeter like curved terribly sharp knife, he would cut it out a sole from a large sheet of thick new leather. He then placed the shoe on an anvil like steel stand and with a mouth full of small nails, would hammer one by one into the sole onto the shoe. Among the clatter of the workshop were scraps of leather of various shades, while recently repaired shoes lined the rack. It was quite exciting to try any new pair of shoes, which were made to order by hand. Sadly they invariably pinched here and there at first.

I was very attached to my mother and was perhaps a bit of a momma's boy, yet I was not spoiled or especially pampered. Throughout the difficult times following our separation, I was very conscious of my mother's spirit, having a strong faith in evoking her protective powers. Later in life, one of my great regrets was that my parents never had the chance to see our children.

Gymnazium

Gymnazium, which was the name of our high school, featured prominently in our daily life. From my early childhood, I was aware of my brothers' progress and the occasional tribulations. I was also well acquainted with their friends and teachers who I would meet on the occasional visits to school or at official or social functions. Both Ludwik and Bob spent

eight years at the school, capping their education by having to write and pass a brutal final examination, known as Matura (matriculation) . I vividly recall how seriously they prepared for this examination. It was a time of great anxiety and no effort was spared to cram in as much learning, as long as the "midnight oil" lasted. At those times, the house was a beehive of fevered activity that affected the whole family for weeks on end. The occasional tutors and communal learning with friends filled our home with nervous energy, suffused with anxiety, but also with a spirit of a warm collegiality. Passing the Matura, especially with good grades, was of paramount importance. Both Ludwig and Bob, some three years apart, passed with grades good enough to be admitted to the universities of their choice. The Higher School of Business in Warsaw, which Ludwig attended for three years from 1936, was already at that time a nest of anti-Semitic behavior. The Christian students would attempt to force their Jewish colleagues to sit on the left side of the lecture hall for symbolic reasons. Such discriminatory attitudes became more pervasive throughout academe in Poland in the second half of the third decade. This was influenced and strengthened by the generally anti-Semitic trends emanating from Germany. No less important was the direction of the new Polish government led by a click of right wing Colonels. They reversed the tolerant internal policies after the death of the previous prime minister and the father of the reconstituted Poland, Marshall Pilsudski.

The refusal by the Jewish students to sit on the designated left side often resulted in fights. The outcome was of course predictable because they were in the minority. Never the less, Ludwik graduated in 1938 and took over a branch of our fathers business in Lodz at the ripe age of 20. He had to obtain an official dispensation to allow for such serious financial undertaking, at such precautious age. He made a spectacular success of it. Regrettably, it lasted only one year because the war broke out on September of 1939. My brother Bob, then known as Noldek, a diminutive of Arnold, was admitted to an engineering college in Birmingham England, just before the onset of the war. It was most fortunate that our mother had relatives there, by the name of Lester. They very graciously invited him to live with them and were most helpful in obtaining a student visa. They also arranged for his admission to an engineering college. I still remember the letter he wrote on his impressions traveling on a train across Germany. He described yellow smoke rising from the many chemical factories

along the way. He felt certain that Germany was preparing seriously for war. Little did he know then, how many millions would have died from the poison manufactured there.

I attended the gymnasium for one year only, but found the curriculum challenging, especially learning math. I found German very difficult at school. Paradoxically, I learned it later with the greatest of ease and I can speak it quite fluently even to this day. Our teachers, who we addressed as professors, were in fact highly educated people. They were committed educators with little if any attrition over the years. Their salaries were pittance, hardly above the poverty line. This was probably in large measure due to the poor state of national economy, coupled with the worldwide depression of the thirties. Yet, they were expected to adhere to middle class values and appearance. Some of them were in need of additional financial help from time to time to which my parents and the other more affluent members of our school community provided. My brothers and I were never at school at the same time because they both were significantly older then I, yet by the time I entered the Gymnasium I was quite familiar with all the teachers. I recall especially, a professor Barbag, with great fondness. He taught physics and math. When as a child I had an occasion to visit my big brother at their school, he always showed interest in me treating me kindly without patronizing. He was even then politically very much to the left. He survived the war in the Soviet Union becoming a high-ranking member of the Communist party on his return to Poland. He also assumed a senior position in the ministry of Education. We met him again when the government entrusted him with a special mission to London in 1946. My brothers and I were delighted that he survived the war and to have the opportunity to meet him again. Not surprising, he felt at that time, that we should all return to Poland; it was a suggestion that was not particularly appealing to any of us. It might be worth mentioning that unlike in prewar Poland, many governmental positions were given to those Jews who were active Communists before the war or escaped to the relative safety of Soviet Russia. These Jews in government were in numbers larger and out of proportion to the rest of the population. The godless Communist government was hardly popular in the country at large at that time, as Poles were staunch Catholics and rabid Russophobes from way back. Later, the Polish government influenced by Stalin's hostile attitude towards the Jews, changed radically. This resulted in a policy of official anti-Semitism which was then eagerly embraced by the civilian

population. This led to some gruesome behavior in a few towns, which could only be adequately described as pogroms. Such brutal expression of anti-Semitism caused the final exodus from Poland of the already decimated Jewish population. From over three million citizens only a few short years before, only a handful of those survived remained in Poland. This was a land which centuries before, unlike many countries where there was a rampant prosecution of the Jews, welcomed them with open arms.

I diverted from describing my life during the first year of my high school year only to give a glimpse of post war Poland. Especially the particular role that Barbag played, as it was emblematic of the futile aspirations for a meaningful role which the surviving Jews like him hoped for, to find in the new Poland. After a year or so of his visit to London, we never heard from him again.

Although I might have been somewhat educationally challenged, I was quite happy in my first year at high school. My cousin Irka with whom I grew up, was in a grade higher than I was. She always included me in her group of friends so I was neither lonely nor unprotected. The wife of the headmaster, Pani Polusiuk, was an exceptionally intelligent, bright, yet charming guiding spirit of the school. Her husband however, was mainly the hands- on administrator. Although it was a very small institution, predominantly Jewish, it was privately supported, generally limited to the middle class children whose parents could afford the tuition. There seemed to be always the threat of fiscal insecurity hanging over the school. Yet there was very little attrition among the faculty, despite the fact that to a man, they all were over qualified to teach at a high school. In those days, it was very difficult to find appropriate positions for the Jewish intelligentsia, no matter how emancipated. Despite its limited recourses, the sciences, math and languages were well taught, as was physical education and theatre which were integral parts of the curriculum. Polish language and its literature were of course intensively taught, as was German and Latin. The latter was the bane of our existence, as we had a very demanding teacher, an utterly harsh and a bitter man feared by all from year one. Each lesson would start with a salutation in Latin "Salve Domine Magister" while the whole class would stand to attention, as he entered the room. Similarly, at the end of the lesson, we would rise up again, reciting in unison "Vale Domine Magister",

as he exited the room. His private life titillated our small community, as he lived with both his wife and their child and a mistress in the same tiny apartment, which was a frequent cause for gossip. The other teachers were mainly single, limited probably by lack of adequate income, although most were very personable and quite attractive. I passed that year with a grade probably equivalent to a C plus. Two months later the war broke out, which was the end of my formal education until we reached South Africa seven years later, in October 1946.

Fragments from Radomsko

Radomsko was similar probably to other small provincial towns where not infrequently one may find a cast of odd or strange characters. The first who comes to mind is Leibele, the water-carrier and his family. They remain a poignant memory, as it led to an early lesson for me in charity and social responsibility. One such incident left me embarrassed to this day. This odd little gnome of a man, mentally challenged to say the least, literally dressed in rags. He was usually seen followed by his wife with a string of five ragamuffins of a gradually diminishing stature, all in an equally semi-naked state of dress. Most of the time, he would be carrying two heavy buckets filled with water suspended from a wooden yoke strung across his shoulders. Although they were often subjected to ridicule, they somehow managed to live on the edge of the community, which barely provided them with token support. They always looked half-starved and were terribly dirty. The incident which I am about to describe happened one early summer day. I was given ten "groshy" for an ice cream, but as I was leaving the store engrossed in my favorite vanilla flavored cone, I ran into the water-carrier and his brood. One of the little boys sneaked behind my elbow and quickly stole a lick of my ice cream. This incensed me to no end, as I was too revolted to keep eating it. In my anger and disgust, I threw it on the pavement rather than giving it to the kid, and then I either hit or pushed the little boy down. Soon after the event, my father somehow heard about it, which lead to a very severe scolding, much deserved in retrospect. It was a good moral lesson for a nine year old, to aim to be kind and generous. It stayed with me for the rest of my life.

I had another experience early on, touching on emotions and human behavior, which lead me to be aware of always showing respect. There was a pathetic but very pretty young woman who was the local prostitute. She always wore very exaggerated make-up, so as children we called her “lalka” or doll. This was meant not as a compliment but rather as derision, especially when as a pack of kids we would occasionally follow her shouting "hey lalka”. One day when she had finally had enough of this derogatory teasing, she chased us through a very narrow alley much to my well-remembered terror. We just managed to escape in the nick of time from what probably would have been a much-deserved thrashing.

There was a tragically comic character, which was a constant source of bemusement for us. This was a member of a well-to-do, respected family in town. He was always elegantly dressed, wearing a freshly pressed gray-striped trousers, an immaculately tailored black jacket with a waistcoat and a bowler hat on his head. He would stride purposely around the town square, swinging a Malacca cane with a silver handle with vigor and an air of great importance. In the other hand, he had with him a substantial leather brief case, contents of which, as we have eventually found out, consisted of potato peals and old newspapers. He obviously suffered from some form of delusion, but proved harmless to the community, most of whom regarded him with some mocking affection.

One of the more pleasant memories of my childhood was the occasional appearance of the street musicians in the courtyard of our building. Among others, I especially recall the song “It was on the isle of Capri that I met you….”. It was such an incongruous sentiment to hear on a gray cold autumn day, imagine being on this lovely balmy island so far way. It must have been the contrast between the sentiment and reality that struck me which is why I remembered it so well. Usually after a number of songs and a few tunes on the fiddle were done, we dropped a few “groshy” (pennies) from the window wrapped in a piece of paper, which the musicians would then catch in their hats with great agility.

The poverty was so pervasive in the general population that our family was economically considered upper middle class. Besides the substantial property in town, we owned a villa in the country, could afford high school, university educations, summer and winter vacations,

and even an occasional foray outside the country, such as my brother Ludwik's trip to the international exposition in Paris. In contrast, the vast majority of the local population was relatively poor with some others barely existing on the edge of privation. Occasionally a few would resort to extreme or unusual measures to supplement their meager earnings. One such case that comes to mind is the tale about the glazier. Our apartment building had some very tall windows over the stairwell, which on occasion, were found broken for no apparent reason. This must have occurred some time during the night, as the damage was discovered usually in the early morning. A day or two later the local glazier would inquire if by chance there was any work for him. When this began to occur with some frequency, suspicions were aroused. Indeed, one day he was observed throwing stones at the windows in the hours of the early dawn. My father looked on such acts as an expression of desperate need, rather than wonton vandalism. We invariably called on the same glazier for the repairs, for which he was paid in a flimsily disguised act of charity.

Dr. Lubelski was our family doctor. He and his very formidable wife Malvina and their three sons also deserve some mention. They belonged to our circle of close friends with whom we were often in daily contact and on occasions, in a need of medical care. Dr. Lubelski was a man short in stature with a military bearing (he was a veteran of the Polish Legion under Marshal Pilsudki, which led to the establishment of a free Republic with the famous pianist Jan Padarewski as its first president. Until then, Poland was partitioned for 150 years into three separate zones administered and dominated by Germany in the west, Austria in the south and the Imperial Russia in the eastern and central part of the country. It might be worth noting that through all this time they retained their language and the Catholic faith despite great pressures by the occupying powers, especially by Russia to Russify the Poles. This, and a vicious armed struggle, which took place soon after the end of World War I between the newly recreated Poland and the young Soviet Union, left a deeply seated enmity between these two nations). Dr. Lubelski was a vigorous man with a warm and charming personality. In contrast his wife was a fullbodied woman with a personality to match. The cobbled stones echoed loudly when she walked the streets of Radomsko. Certainly to a young mind as mine, she was not to be trifled with lightly. Yet I was glad whenever I had a chance to go with my mother to visit them, as Pani Malwina was a phenomenal cook. Her

Achilles' heel, however, was her well founded jealousy of her husband's fondness for young women, which was legendary. This often lead to gossip, causing much merriment and snickering about his various escapades, which invariably led to a subsequent punishment meted out with vigor by Pani Malwina. The saga of the Lubelski family if detailed could have easily served as a text for a Roman a Clef, if all their many adventures were tallied. Except for Pani Malvina, they all survived the war in Siberia. On the return to Poland, Dr,Lubelski and his son, a gynecologist(whose divorced wife and young son Nana and I met again in Montreal)resumed their respected practices. The other son Mietek, a contemporary and friend of Uncle Ludwik's became vice minister for coal, while Lolek the third son, a reprobate in his younger days and a friend of uncle Bobs', was a high ranking officer in the Polish army. After Dr..Lubelski died, all three sons settled in Germany, where according to Uncle Ludwik, they prospered in some very questionable enterprise.

The Happy Days of Summer

Before I leave my childhood behind, I must include some recollections of the happy summers, which I was privileged to spend, in our villa in Kaminsko. In my adolescence, which preceded the war, I spent the summer in sleep away camps, in the mountains of the Tatras and Pieniny regions, of southern Poland. For me these last three summers, provided especially exciting and a rewarding experience, which in fact contributed greatly to my early physical and intellectual development.

Kaminsko was a sleepy little hamlet situated about seven miles from Radomsko. It not only symbolized the joys and leisure of the summer months, but also was light years removed from the humdrum daily responsibilities of the rest of the year. I truly loved spending the long vacation, there. What was especially exciting for me, which I awaited with great anticipation each year, were the extensive preparations and packing for the journey. And indeed the was a journey was considerable undertaking, in spite of the rather short distance between Radomsko and the village of Kaminsko, considering that the mode of transportation then was a horse drawn wagon. It was loaded with mounds of household stuff for the two months or so of our stay in the villa. It required much planning and effort by my mother and

our maid Bella. Huge trunks like wicker baskets were loaded with bedding, linen, cutlery and other assorted gear including clothing. As a special favor I would be allowed to sit next to the driver. On some occasions he would let me hold the reigns, and for a short time, under his close watch, I would be allowed to lead the horses.

Our property consisted of a substantial garden, a rather large two-storied halftimbered Tudor-like villa and four acres of forest. It was a narrow property, so it seemed very long. It front was near a railway line some distance away on one side, ending at the other alongside a road on the main route to Warsaw. The thick forest of tall pines with rich undergrowth was mysterious and enchanting.

Our family usually occupied the top floor that had a fine vine shaded veranda. The lower part of the villa was rented out, usually to some family friends, so I never lacked playmates. There was a separate small dwelling for the permanent overseer and his wife. I have fond memories of them both. They were very kind to me, but in particular I liked eating with them. His wife would invite me for a typical Polish peasant soup cooked with tiny bits of bacon, well-browned onions, and potatoes. There was a modest round shaped garden in the front of the villa and an orchard behind, with a gazebo, overgrown with sweetly scented jasmine. A little ways to the left of the house bordering on the edge of the forest, was the well remembered, but the indispensable double privy. To a small child especially in the dark, the way there seemed not only awfully long, but also inhabited I feared, by demons or bogymen. It was especially difficult, when as a result of eating unripe fruit, a major stomach upset usually meant having to swallow the inevitable dose of castor oil, with predictable results. During the day, the woods were truly magical. We gathered wild strawberries (fraise de bois), blueberries and blackberries, which if not eaten before we reached home, would be shared with others, with the addition of sweeten whipped cream. At times, we would also venture to gather wild mushrooms, especially after good rains have fallen. On other occasions a group of friends and I would dig a hole to bake potatoes. We filled it with dry the pine branches, then tried to light a fire, by rubbing two flint stones. When the cinders got good and hot, then was the time, to finally, bake the potatoes. What fun it was to eat them with little salt, skin and all. To this day, I recall their special charred taste. In the orchard, in

the early summer, when all other trees were still hung up with unripe fruit, we had one apple tree, which bore apples much sooner than others did. I have never seen or tasted this type of apple anywhere else. It had gentle, but refined taste, with a rather light texture and a very pleasant scent. It was called "papierowka", which meant to describe this apple to be as light as paper. Another special memory from the summers there was the occasion when the roof needed fresh paint of tar. While I liked the smell of hot tar, I also enjoyed making black rivulets with it in the sand. This was not especially appreciated by my mother, as it invariably resulted in soiling my clothing, hands and feet, which were hard to clean.

Kamisko was surrounded by large pine forests and tracts of sandy soil, where potatoes, blue legumes, and wheat grew in abundance. There were invariably children of various ages around, so I never lacked playmates. As the summer progressed, we picked the blue cornflower in the fields of ripening grain, to make garlands. I was especially friendly with Stefa and Dzidka Kreindler. The latter of course you have known as uncle Ludwik's wife. The other frequent companion was Bronka Kirschenbaum. I knew her since my early childhood and we remained friends throughout our isolation in the Radomsko Ghetto. We lost contact after the dissolution of the Ghetto, only to pick it up again, after the war. It was first by letter from her when we were in London, then much later when Edith and I left for Canada, we stopped to see her in New York. By then she Married Adam Novak and had a six-month-old daughter Linda. It was so thrilling, to find after so many turbulent years, such a close friend from my early childhood. In particular, seeing the little child of Bronka's was particularly poignant for me, at that time. The presence of this new generation was singularly symbolic of our survival, in spite of the past horrors. When we moved to New York we met frequently, but whenever we saw each other, mixed memories abounded, steeped in nostalgia and spiked with high emotions. Sadly, I was also a witness when Bronka, on three separate occasions, faced a life-threatening illness. I am mentioning this only, because each time I was involved either peripherally or directly in her care. The first instance was in the Ghetto, when she developed bacterial meningitis. We all were very sad, as she was not expected to survive. Somehow, the new Sulfa drugs were procured with the help of the head of the Jewish police in Warsaw. He was the Kirschenbaums' former neighbor and a notorious German collaborator. Despite this severe illness, she survived to the jubilation of her friends. Later,

when I was only in New York five months, I received a call from her that she was not well. Adam was out of town and she could not get a doctor, because the Jewish high holidays just started .When I arrived in their apartment in Queens, I found her in bed, seriously ill. It was not much of a challenge for me to diagnose a ruptured ectopic pregnancy. She had the classic signs and symptoms of severe internal bleeding. I was fortunate to be able finally to locate her gynecologist, as she declined my offer to take her by ambulance to Jacoby Hospital. She recovered well enough after an emergency operation and blood transfusions, to get pregnant once more, when her daughter Karen was born some years later. Unfortunately, the third major illness proved fatal within six weeks of diagnosis of a rapidly growing breast cancer. Here too I was involved in the initial phase, but only for a moral support. She was sadly missed by all who knew her.

It was with Bronka that I had many exciting escapades in Kamisko, and later during our existence in the Ghetto. She was little older than I. She was very pretty and usually the leader of the pack. On sunny days, we would venture on long hikes to the local river, to picnic or swim. One day we were caught there, in a severe thunderstorm. The only possible shelter from the rain, but obviously not from the fierce lightning bolts all around us, was an iron railway tresel. It was one of those unintended childhood experiences, as iron, being a good conductor of electricity it was hardly a save haven. Other favorite activity was to go on long hikes in to the surrounding forests, where we would visit the local peasants. It was always someone, who one of us knew. They lived in the forest in primitive cottages with mud floors with a few little windows and a thatch roof. Some even kept their few animals with them inside the hut. Yet they were very hospitable. For a special treat, they offered freshly boiled new potatoes with sour milk, which was coated with a layer of the yellow cream. Sometimes, they let us help churn the cream, when they were making butter. We would then not leave until it was all done, so we could drink the remaining fresh buttermilk, which was the fat free residue, after the formed butter was removed. It contained however, the occasional tiny golden specks of butter residue. It tasted so much better, than the one found in stores these days. Those peasant women we visited, were the same who came regularly to the villa, selling wild berries, mushrooms eggs or fresh butter, wrapped in a moisten linen, with beads of water sweating through the cloth. They carried these in a homemade wicker

basket, covered with a thick blanket or a shawl. For a short time, fresh strawberries and cherries were available directly from the local gardeners. Then toward the end of the summer, the hazel nuts, which grew along one of our fences ripened. The local country store, to us as children, was always very exciting, not only because of the infinite variety of goods and candies, but because it was the only place near by which had freshly made ice cream. Once a week, was an eagerly awaited arrival from Radomsko of our bagel baker. Each summer she arrived by train with a tray full of freshly backed pastries to sell to the vacationers like us. We were only permitted to choose one. The allure of a creampuff sprinkled lightly with a confectionery sugar, or a tort like pastry or best of all a small blue berry pie, oozing sticky black syrup from its sides, presented no small dilemma of choice, for a small boy. This poor women in an effort to earn a few groshy (pennies) would bring these goodies to us on a metal tray covered in the heat of summer, with a woolen shawl, draped over her shoulders. How hygienic it all was then, I dare not think now. I was particularly fond of her not only for these weekly summer treats, but also for another reason. I discovered and understood later, this woman was actually my wet nurse, when for some reason my mother could not breast-feed me. Through out my childhood she was kind and showed interest in me. I would always be glad to have an opportunity to visit with her. Not infrequently, I was sent to buy fresh hot bagels from her, which was more of an act of charity than a real need. I treasure the memories of the summers in Kaminsko, far more so than those years of my life in Radomsko.

Summers in the Mountains

Summer at the sleep away camp began each year with a long train journey south. I looked forward to meeting other campers and making new friends. The arrival of the train in the late hours of the evening, the huge locomotive coming slowly to a stop, hissing clouds of steam, set the level of excitement at a high threshold. The train compartment crowded with equally exited children who welcomed the new arrivals with great gusto. This scene was repeated at several stations down the line, as the campers came from various parts of the country. The night was spent talking, singing, exchanging introductions, doing every thing but sleeping, till we would arrive bleary eyed, to our destination the following morning. On arrival we

would form a long line of three or four abreast march to the camp. If the camp was situated some distance from the railroad station, we were then driven there in the horse drawn, long wooden farm wagons. We would usually sit, five or six, on either side of the cart with our legs swinging to the rhythm of the wheels. The trick was not to get ones feet caught in their spokes. Once having arrived there, the first order of the day was to find the assigned housing and to fix the beds and bedding. This was not as simple as it might sound. First we were issued two jute sacks, the larger one to be filled with coarse straw to serve as mattress and smaller to be filled with sweet smelling hay to serve for a pillow. The linen to complete the bed we brought with us from home. The beds consisted of a rough wooden frame with several loose narrow planks of wood to support the straw mattress. Much sport was had when we discovered that by removing a few of those planks from the center the mattress would fall to the floor, with the unsuspected victim of the prank in it.

It was a coeducational camp run by secular Jewish newspaper, printed in Polish by the name of Nasz Przeglond (Our Review). Its editorial board was Socialist in its political outlook. The camp director was a highly regarded authority in geography on an international level. He was a heavyset man with a neck deeply pitted with old acne scars, He was a very enlightened and supporting mentor. The underlying mantra of the camp was "Mens Sano in Corporo Sano" (Healthy Mind in a Healthy Body). Thus we had the opportunity for both intellectual as well as physical growth. The age spread of the campers from eleven to eighteen meant that that even the youngest were made to participate in serious intellectual or political discussions, without being patronized. Similarly all were included in various sport activities or took part on long hikes, to the countryside or to the mountains. We were made to live in a much simpler manner than we were used to at home, removed the usual comforts of our middle class life. Although the children came from many parts of the country, the largest group was from Warsaw. This lent a special the tenor to the camp,as they were far more sophisticated than the rest of us. The first summer I spent in this camp, I was there with my brother Bob. Here I must digress to relate another of those unexpected coincidences of life, as it was then when we apparently met Adam Novak, the future husband of Bronka Kirschenbaum, who featured prominently in the early years of my life and whom I mentioned before. When Bob came to visit us in the States so many years later, it was Adam

who remembered that they used to play ping-pong together. It was a very unexpected reunion, as Adam lived used in Warsaw, where he survived the holocaust with his family with the help of Christian Poles. They were hidden in a small space behind a cupboard, for about two and half years. The strange aspect of this story is the fact that he and Bronka only met for the first time in America. It is remarkable that we knew each of them separately, long before they met each other, but especially, that each of us was somehow lucky enough to survive at all.

I have happy memories recalling my camp experience in my first year there. I happened to be the youngest of all the participants that year, so I was given special privileges and was treated kindly by the other campers and the councilors. When we would venture on prolonged hikes in to mountainous countryside, I would be assigned as the pace maker to march in front of the group.

One outing in particular left a lasting impression on me when we were taken on a rafting trip on the river Poprad, which flows along the Polish- Czech border. It flows between peaks of lime stone outcroppings and this is a fairly narrow, shallow, briskly running river. The raft consisted of several long narrow wooden hulls strung together with ropes. A sitting bench for tourists was placed in the back across all the hulls, while the "goral" (the mountain man), who like the Venetian goodlier, propelled and directed the raft, with a long wooden pole. While passing a bend in the river, the absolute quiet would suddenly be shattered unexpectedly by the mournful notes of a gypsy song. A fiddler up to his waist in the river would appear dressed in motley but colorful dress, with a bandana on his head. The women folk would then collect a few "groshy" thrown with great flourish, by the tourists. If the raft were to stop briefly, the Gypsy women were quick to harass the tourists by insisting to tell them their fortune. A small gypsy encampment with painted wagons was nearby on the banks of the river, while the invariable smoky campfire and grazing horses among the happily running children, completes the picture. No matter how romantic this must seem now, there was serious prejudice against the Gypsies. They were considered not only to be horse thieves but even children thieves (kidnappers is not a word in the Polish lexicon). In fact their main occupations, were begging, fortune telling and making cooper pots. The bad reputation was

so pervasive, that we as children gave them a wide birth. Terrible injustice meted out these people as a group, who like the Jews, were rounded up and exterminated en mass, by the Nazi Germany, during the European Holocaust.

The second summer the camp was situated in a very well known resort of Zakopane, in the Tatra Mountains of southern Poland. Zakopane or Deeply Berried, as its name implies in Polish, was surrounded by high Alpine peaks. Although the camp was, outside the resort proper, we had an easy access to the countryside, which provided opportunities for many hikes. One of the most memorable excursions was the trip to Morskie Oko, a deep clear Alpine lake, which was surrounded by vertically rising peaks of great beauty. We also went tracking in the high Tatras, which was very challenging, and equally exciting.

The third and last summer was spent in the mountains bordering on Romania, but the time was cut in half, because of the political uncertainty and unrest. We returned to Radomsko one month earlier than planed, due to the rapidly rising tensions between Poland and Germany. I say we, because this time your aunt Dzidka was entrusted to my care for this particular summer vacation. As it turned out it was a very lucky decision on the part of the camp administration as other wise, these few hundred children, of which the camp was comprised, would have probably been unable to be reunited with their parents, as the war broke out on the first of September.

The War Years

The Winds of War

It is August of 1939 and the poisonous harangues of Hitler were being heard with an increasing frequency on the German radio. At first such venom, which was directed at Jews primarily, began to include Poland as a whole. The winds of war were clearly at our back. Eventually the question was not if, but when would the hostilities between these two countries break out and indeed they did on this fateful, gloriously beautiful September morning, with a cloudless blue sky above. It was then that I heard the ominous sounds of cannons in the far distance and I have realized that the war has began. Although there was as yet no official announcement, it soon became obvious when the wounded began arriving in the town square. Radomsko, which was fairly near the German-Polish border was among the many places which were attacked by the German Luftwaffe that morning. Lead by the curiosity of a newly minted thirteen-year-old boy I ventured farther into town when a wave of Stukas swarmed overhead. Although un- afraid at first, I managed to duck under the eves of a building, when the raid started in earnest. Those unique diving bombers did not only drop bombs and strafe with the machine gun fire from their wings, but were especially designed to demoralize the enemy. During their sharp decent, they emitted a sustained, frightful sound resembling a siren like screech of great intensity.(Ironically, the Polish Hussars were the first ones, who in the Eighteenth Century have developed similar war tactics to demoralize the confronting enemy. They wore large Angle like wings on their backs made of long feathers in a metal frame. During a fast gallop, the air in the wing created a loud frightening noise ahead, long before they reached the ranks of the enemy).

The air raid on Radomsko, which I am sure must have also occurred in many other locations, foreshadowed the future Nazi tactics of aiming the war primarily at the civilian population. The Polish Air force in which we had such great faith was not in evidence that day. The heroic Polish army was no match for the heavily armed Panzer divisions of the modern German army. There was hardly any contest when a saber-armed legionnaire on a horseback, faced a heavily armed tank. The result was a forgone conclusion, yet those of us within the

maelstrom hoped at the outset, that not only Poland would be able to defend itself, but would emerge victorious in the end. Well the end was long coming. This undeclared, unprovoked invasion under false pretences, lead to the Cataclysm of World War II. Great Britain and France honored their defense pact with Poland and on 3 September reaffirmed their alliance against Nazi Germany. The formal declaration of war was preceded by an ultimatum, issued by the Allies to the Germans, to withdraw from Poland or they would officially join the hostilities. Predictably, Hitler had no such intentions.

My father having recognized the inevitability of German invasion decided that we must leave immediately, because of the proximity of the border. By the time I reached home, shaken somewhat by experience of my first air raid that morning, all the preparations for leaving, were already made. Father managed somehow, to rent a truck with a driver and we piled whatever possessions were at hand. We left Radomsko on the afternoon of the first day of September. The objective was to cross the river Wisla (Vistula) ahead of the Germans. This prominent river dissected Poland in half within its the pre-war borders. It originated in the springs of the Tatras (Carpetian mountains) in the south meandering like a letter "S" to flow out into the Baltic in the north. Apparently our goal was to reach the town of Lublin, a major regional center in the eastern part of the country. The first part of the journey was unimpeded, as most the population farther away from the front were not, as aware of the acute danger, as we were. That night we spent in a hotel at very nice resort. I think we must have stayed there for at least another day, before proceeding farther east. I recall very clearly the pleasant surroundings, even riding my bike or munching on some very special local rolls. This respite allowed my parents to get a more accurate assessment of the situation. When we finally left this place, this time however, the going was very slow, as the roads now were crowded with the fleeing masses. Many were on foot with bundles on their back with the children dragging behind. Others in horse drawn carts, piled high with their life possessions and a few like us, lucky enough to be motorized. I do not recall under what circumstances, but I know that somehow we had to abandon our truck, with most of the staff on it. The roads became progressively more congested, reducing the progress eastwards to a crawl. It was a most beautiful fall that year. Clear days, cloud free skies, the fields of ripening wheat, were in such contrast to the misery of the escaping masses. What made matters worst, were the

occasional strafing sorties of the German Luftwaffe which would suddenly appear out of no where, flying low while shooting at random at the defenseless civilians. The resultant panic of the people and the horses is hard to describe. There was an immediate halt to any movement forward, with people jumping into the shallow ditches, which run on either side of the road, sometime with an only vain attempt to safety.

How or when we finally reached Lublin I have no clear recollection, but by the time we arrived there, the Germans had caught up with us. At the same time, the Soviet Union, by the perfidious betrayal of political morality, also invaded Poland. The Russians occupied the remaining eastern part of the country, now sharing an agreed border directly with the Germans. Thus after only twenty-one years of independence, Poland a country of thirty three million people was once more wiped off the map. This perverse common cause with Nazi Germany would later cause the Russians to suffer twenty million dead and an untold destruction and misery.

The situation in Lublin was very fluid and for a time it was possible to cross over the newly formed border, to the Russian side, which so many of the Jews decided to do. This was not however, an option for my father, for a number of reasons. I, on the other hand at the age of thirteen, was adamant against the family return to Radomsko, as it meant remaining under the Nazi yoke. This family conflict; my first youthful rebellion remains for me, a deeply embedded, bitter memory. To this day, I vividly recall throwing myself on to the bed, kicking wildly on the mattress in a hysterical tantrum, in a protest and sheer frustration. In tears, I shouted that I am not going back. Even the short exposure in Lublin, to the attitude of the regular German soldiers of the Wehrmacht, I sensed their uncompromising disregard and hostility, especially toward the Jews. This made me very fearful for the future and that was well before any exposure to the vicious members of the "SS" or "SD", the specialized police force. This outburst of mine, was the first of such instinctive decisions, which I was forced to make throughout the war, which might have proven to be right.

My father, however, had many rational reasons to go back. His hard earned wealth, accumulated over a lifetime, was in Radomsko. When we left, the warehouse was filled to

the brim with cases of nails, screws and bales upon bales of wire. Anticipating the conflict between Poland and Germany, he was convinced that fiscal safety was in material good, rather than in money, which could fall prey to inflation, which was his experience in the first World War. More importantly making the decision to return home was the unknown fate of my brother Ludwik, whom my parents presumed might have remained in Lodz. Another reason why my father was reluctant to cross over to the Soviet side, was the pervasively hostile attitude of the Communist dogma to anybody they considered a capitalist, which they regarded as the enemy of the state and the common good. At the back of my fathers mind were also the memories of the brutal excesses of the Russian Revolution in contrast to the rather benign German occupation during World War I. Therefore, in the end he might have been more afraid of the Russian Communists than the Germans. This proved to be a fatal choice. The majority of Jews who found themselves in Soviet occupied part of Poland or crossed over there, in early days of the war, have survived, in spite of great hardships ,when they were resettled later, into the hostile vastness of eastern Russia or Siberia. In contrast, those Jews who remained under the German occupation were decimated. Some few who have survived did so under assumed identity or remained hidden for several years under the most difficult circumstances. There were a handful of others who managed come out of the concentration camps but barely alive. These were those who either by luck or wit were placed in such camps, which were designated for the German war effort, such the ammunition manufacture or building fortifications. They too, lived or rather existed under the most appalling conditions, which also lead to many deaths.

The Long Trek Home and the Aftermath

The only way for us to get back to Radomsko was to travel on the back roads, in a farmer's wooden wagon with its wooden wheels rimmed by steel bands, drawn by a single horse. We felt every jolt of the wheels on the corrugated surface of these rough country roads. The vagrancy of the autumn weather in the open, unprotected farmers cart added to our general discomfort. Worst of all was the uncertainty of what might be awaiting us on our return. I was especially sorry for my mother, who had to endure the discomforts and indignities of

such protracted journey, under these circumstances. Whatever belongings we had, were somehow lost on the way. My beautiful red bicycle given to me on my thirteenth birthday was long gone. Within a space of weeks, we were reduced to a life of the Gypsies. Occasionally we would join others in similar circumstances when we formed a long line of wagons, riding together for protection. Once we came across a troop the German soldiers, who called us derisively the "Juden caravan". Another time, in this sketchily remembered journey, we arrived in an early evening at a small Jewish village, known generically as a "Shtetle", which were especially common in the eastern part of Poland. This must have been during the Jewish High Holiday, as we were invited to their festive meal and were given lodging for the night. Before then I hardly knew that such isolated, predominantly Jewish villages even existed. Finally, when we reached our hometown one the late afternoon we found the apartment intact and undisturbed. Soon after, our family friend, the accountant Mr. Kirschenbaum* arrived to greet us and without any preamble informed my father that all the commodities so carefully amassed in our warehouses before the war, were either looted or confiscated by the Germans. My father's fortune; the fruits of a life long labor, enterprise and careful planning were lost without redemption. I recall vividly this very moment of disbelieve and shock registered on his ashen gray face, as he collapsed into a chair, in utter despair. It was there and then that I resolved never to become a businessman, but try to choose other means of livelihood. I would rather be a lowly tradesman with manual skills, of which one cannot be robed, so easily.

For the time being we remained in our home, but had to endure repeatedly, the indignities of the unwelcome intrusions by the local Volksdeusche (Poles of German origin) who were given a free hand to steal and plunder, especially from the Jews. They would enter our home at will, picking up any object of furniture or any other of our possessions, which they may fancy. I was particularly sad to lose my divan-like bed. It was given it as a special present, just before the war. It was handmade of highly polished wood with a glass bookcase at its head. To add insult to injury, I had to witness some gross behavior while they tested the bed by bouncing up and down while making obscene remarks. This divan and the red bicycle were my pride and joy. I was to lose them both.

We remained in our apartment until the ghetto was formerly opened after a series of proclamations by the German authorities forcing all the Jews on the pain of severe punishment, to move into segregated enclosed area. No provisions were made however to find the corresponding housing for the displaced families. Each had to find a new place to live in the already inadequate designated part or town. My father managed to rent a part of a small cottage, which we shared with the owner Mr. Jaworski and his family. Although they were Christians, they were allowed for the time being to live side by side, despite the fact that the cottage was incorporated into the confines of the newly established Ghetto. The cottage stood on a property, which contained a rather substantial vegetable garden at the end of which was a large barn. A smaller area in the front contained a fruit orchard. Overall, it was a substantial property, enclosed by a high wooden fence on all sides. Thus, ironically we had a large measure of privacy, denied for most part to the rest of the population of the Ghetto. We lived in relative harmony with the owner, his wife and their two adolescent children, until eventually further restrictions forced them out onto the Christian side of the town. I think, that it might have been Mr. Jaworsky who arranged for our potential hiding place in the barn, which allowed us as a family to avoid the first major action and the subsequent transport to the extermination camps.

The main gate of the Ghetto abutted the beginning of our property. Facing us, on the other side of the road, were the buildings of Judenrat or the administrative offices of the Jewish Board of Deputies. These men were designated by German authorities for the administration of the Ghetto on their behalf. They were also ordered to create and supervise the Jewish Police force, who except for uniforms and batons, carried no arms. Although the board in part was composed of some previously eminent members of the community, they were there to do the Nazi's bidding. As it turned out later, they became in the end the Judas' goats. My father was approached to join the board, but he rightly declined to be involved in this ethically questionable administration, although belonging to it had its benefits.

I could never understand how my father managed to the very end have enough money to support us, even in these modest circumstances, without any sustained source of income, for three and a half years. Hiding the cash and valuables was a challenge with both the need to

secrecy and the potential for rapid retrieval, if such an occasion should arise. One ingenious place, which amused me no end, was the use of the home heating stove. These were the erect, tall rectangular stoves made of thick but hollowed tiles, which conducted the heat generated by burning coal in enclosed grate at the bottom. Once the fire was lit, a solid iron door was closed, allowing for a slow burn, which retained the heat for hours. In the morning grate was clean of the ash. As the actual fire was limited to the grate in the lower part of the stove, there was no danger even for the paper money to catch fire. A tile, one usually chosen from the upper part of the stove, was very carefully removed and the valuables were placed in its capacious hollow space. The tile was then carefully replaced and sealed with fresh grit. The trick of course was to remember which one among the many tiles was the one containing the valuables. Were it not for the money and the diamond broach given to me on our last parting by my parents, I would not have any material means of survival.

*Mr. Kirschenbaum was the father of my friend Bronka, later known as Betty Novak whom I describe elsewhere.

The Ghetto and the "Final Solution"

The life in the Ghetto was characterized by a progressive limitation on personal freedoms, the availability of food, medicines and a general deprivation of goods for daily needs. As the war progressed the Germans ratcheted the emotional and material conditions to a point of despair. I will avoid describing the daily life in this hermetically closed Ghetto, as there is a very moving, a rather accurate diary by one of my contemporaries, Miriam Chaszczewacki, the Polish Ann Frank. I encourage you to read the book by Stefania Kreindler Heilbrun , entitled "Children of Dust and Heaven". It was inspired by Miram's diary, the original of which, written in Polish, now rests in the archives of Yad Vashem. It may be of interest that Stefa Kreindler was one of my childhood friends, who later became, uncle Ludwik's sister in law. I hope that this book will serve as an important companion piece to my memoir. It attests powerfully to a vivid eye witnesses' despair of the times and also describes briefly, the life in prewar Radomsko; has also maps and photographs which might be of interest.

I will therefore focus narrowly, on my personal experience. I cannot leave my early life in the Ghetto without, however, mentioning the two persons who for a short time made my existence there bearable. One was my Grandmother who lived with us for some time, but died long before the Ghetto was eliminated. The other was my cousin, a boy slightly older than I, who stayed with us there, for a short time. His name was Ludwik Jakubowicz who before the war lived in Katowice. It was there, that I used to spend my winter vacations, often at his home. I remember him with great affection because of those times together. He would take me to all the films in town, because his father by being an executive of the "Paramount" film studio, had free tickets to all the local cinemas. I especially treasure the memory of the days he spent with us in the Ghetto. He made me listen to music and encouraged me to read. To this day, I remember the opening notes of the Second Hungarian Rhapsody by List, which he played on a hand wound phonograph. He also had a smattering of English, so he taught me such unrelated phrases as "you silly goose" or "psychology of crowds". To my regret, he soon left us, to rejoin his immediate family, all whom I must presume, were killed.

In the fall of 1942, there were rumors of forced resettlements of the Jews through out Poland to so-called labor camps. At no time were we aware that this was a subterfuge disseminated by the German propaganda to dissuade the people from any potential resistance, even though arms were hardly available. It was October and the Radomsko Ghetto was overcrowded beyond capacity, as it had to absorb those Jews who were expelled from the neighboring villages and small towns. Although there was pervasive sense of doom, I really cannot recall in all honesty, that there was any clear awareness at that time, that we might be facing an inescapable or imminent death. As a family, we have resolved however, to remain in Radomsko at all cost and try to avoid a possible transport to what appeared to be a forced labor camps.

I do not recall how it came about that Mr. Jaworski, who owed the property on which we then lived, has prepared a hiding place for us in the barn at the other end of the garden. As a Christian Pole, he must have first had to overcome the restrictions of even entering the Ghetto. I wonder if he knew more of what we were about to face? The first most comprehensive "action", a euphemism the Germans used for describing herding people out

of their homes in preparation for transport to the concentration camps, began in the early hours of that day of doom. As our cottage was near the main gate of the Ghetto, we were awaken by the harsh, metallic noise of the military vehicles and the very large transport lorries which followed, accompanied by the Germans and the Polish Police. Especially ominous were the bright lights penetrating the dark mist of an early dawn. I was struck by the sight of the wide-open gates at the entrance of the Ghetto, which appeared to me in that light, as the gates of hell. I have immediately alerted my parents of the imminent danger. We have grabbed some minimal provisions and run to the hiding place in the barn. This consisted of a very narrow space between thick wooden beams of the first floor of the barn which, when covered with heavy wooden planks, formed a false space. The floor was then masked with a pile of straw. Somebody must have helped us to hide, but how and who I cannot recollect. We had to lie down in this barely wide enough narrow space head to toe. We had no water, only some scraps of bread, and for some unexplained reason, we had a single lemon. This sustained us for about thirty-six hours or so. As the action continued through out this long day of doom, we could hear a progressively louder tumult arising from the neighboring soccer field across from the road. Apparently the Germans used this large open space for the" Versamlungplatz" (Assembly Square), to which they brutally horded the people from their homes, an mass. From there, they were taken by large tracks to the local train station for farther transport in the cattle cars, to an unknown destination. It was only after the war, that I found out that it was the infamous Treblinka. By the evening, the noise and commotion has gradually subsided. I think that it was the early afternoon of that day, when we heard the Germans entering the barn, by which time we were already thoroughly terrified. Eventually they found their way to the top floor, where we laid hidden numbed by fear. We could hear them shuffling around in search directly over our heads, conscious of every step they made in their nail hobbled boots. There was hardly any space between our bodies and the heavy wooden planks, which would give in slightly under the weight of the search group, making it for us even harder to breath. Or was it fear that held our breath? I am sure that they brought dogs with them too, as we heard barking. To our total disbelieve and an enormous relief, they failed somehow to find us. (I must divert here, to alert you, that if you ever will see the film Schindler's List, an identical situation to ours was portrayed in a scene which depicted the action of herding the Jews from the Krakow Ghetto. In the film the family however, is

discovered in their hiding place, we in contrast remained somehow miraculously undetected) As the evening progressed the strange, overpowering noise which has emanated from the many thousands of anxious, frighten people gradually subsided as the "Versamlung Platz" was finally emptied. That meant that, some twelfth to fifteen thousand men, women and children, were in a space of a single day were systematically and brutally uprooted from their homes, with little if any possessions, overwhelmed by fear of what the future might hold.

It was sometime later in the following day that we ventured to look outside. As we emerged from the gray darkness of the barn, I was almost blinded by the brilliant sunshine of a clear October day. I was struck by a strangely eerie silence surrounding us. Stepping outside the barn, I noticed an old worn out horseshoe under my foot. I instantly picked it up and pitched it over my left shoulder, remembering the local peasants' superstition who believed that it would bring good luck. This was the first of a number of strange and baffling events, which border on the mystic, which I encountered on several other occasions. Perhaps it is not surprising that I became deeply superstitious for the rest of my life.

It was in the afternoon of the following day when we finally emerged from our hiding in the Barn for good. We stopped at our cottage only long enough, to collect some belongings. At first, as looked over the fence of our property, we saw no people; we then cautiously opened the gate on to the street and very quietly ventured directly across the road to the building housing the Jewish Board (Juderat) responsible to the Germans for administrating the Ghetto. To our surprise, we found our selves among about one hundred and fifty or so survivors of the action. Only the days before, there were well over ten thousand people in this Ghetto. This small group was mostly comprised of those Jews who were the members of the Board of Deputies and the Jewish Police. They were used by the Germans to administer the Ghetto. There was also small group of people, who like us, somehow managed to avoid the initial deportation action. I suspect, that the members of the board and the police were made to collaborate in this first action. Throughout the existence of the Ghetto, some members of these two groups benefited materially from such collaboration materially. They also might have hoped that by this, in the end they would have had a chance to save them selves and or their families .For most it was a spurious hope, for others, especially those who were in high

positions, however some have somehow, managed to survive the war, as did some members of their families.

I think that we remained in the buildings of the Jewish Board, for only a few days, before the next action took place. In the mean time, we ate at a communal kitchen, slept in a large hall, crowded with all others, on the floor, in full dress with our boots on, with the little of what remained of our belongings cradling next to us anticipating future actions father decided to seek out a more reliable hideout, but this time it was to be outside the confines of the Ghetto walls. We have joined a small group of others who apparently knew of such a place. How we even managed to get there undetected, in that particular part of town, in a bright daylight I cannot fathom. I am quite certain that it was in the neighborhood of our old home, on Pilsudski Street. We were lead to a small vaulted cellar, which after we entered, was sealed outside by bricks and mortar. How we were expected to survive without any access to ventilation, was either terribly naïve or wicked. I suspect that whoever provided this opportunity for us to hide, by pretending to help, was in fact either planning to denounce us to the Germans, or more likely expected us to die and then loot whatever money and valuables were in our possession. I recall very clearly to this day, being overwhelmed by an intense panic and claustrophobia, the moment I entered the cellar and the wall was sealed. Within a very short time I have realized, that in fact, we were in a hopeless situation, so with out the permission of others, I decided to break out from the cellar. I also noticed that a boy slightly older than, who I knew had Tuberculosis, began to cough up blood. He and I began pushing out the bricks with our bare hands. Fortunately the still fresh mortar presented no significant resistance. As we were frantically pushing the bricks out, to make an exit hole in the wall, I noticed bloody sputum splattered over my bear arms and hands. I am astounded, that I have not become infected myself at the time. More over I am certain that I probably had a low resistance to infection because of the prolonged period of poor nutrition and the severe stress caused by the recent events. Once out of there, having looked carefully around, we made our way back to the confines of the Ghetto. On the way, as we proceeded very cautiously, I have noticed under nave of a house a ceramic figure of the Virgin Mary holding Baby Jesus, although being neither religious nor a Catholic, I felt a desperate need to pray invoking their blessing for our salvation.

The next few days, after our return to the confines of the Ghetto, were spent in an anxious anticipation of the inevitable future actions. On one such occasion, I had strange experience, almost an epiphany. It was a cold, clear, starry evening when all of the few remaining young men were called to assembly by the Germans for a possible work detail. While waiting in line, I incidentally looked up at sky, when for the first time in my life, I became aware of a grouping of stars in a form of a wagon, pointing upwards. I took as an omen that perhaps by going away from Radomsko, leaving the Ghetto, was possibly the sole path to survival. It was only well after the war, when I learned, that this was a well known constellation as the Big Dipper. Throughout my life, I got great pleasure, whenever I would sight it in the northern sky. I considered it my lucky stars, because in fact it was the decision to leave Radomsko, which lead to my survival. Not long after the failed attempt to seek a possible refuge, having rejoined the small group of Jewish officials, and other civilians, who avoided deportation till now, we were faced with another action. As soon I sow the German police and the SS arriving at the gates of the Ghetto, I urged my Parents to try hiding in a deserted Barracks, behind the Judenrat building. It was as naïve, as it was of no avail. My parents, some other adults and the few remaining children were all taken to the local jail, in the preparation for transport to the railway station. I have learned years later, that their destination was the notorious extermination camp of Tremblinka, some sixty miles west of Warsaw.

On the visit to Poland, in 1988 we were taken there, Edith and I, by our driver on a clear evening in May. In the fading light, we were the only people there. It was all so eerie. Just before a most inconspicuous gate, there were a few remaining railway tracts, on which those many transport trains would arrive, with the countless victims in a journey from hell, only to face even a worse fate there. As soon as we entered the camp proper, we encountered roughly hewed groupings of rocks of granite of various sizes. The largest rocks represented the countries, the ones of an intermediate size, the various cities, and the more numerous small rocks symbolized the many little towns and villages from where about one million Jews, Gypsies and Others were killed in a mass slaughter, at Treblinka. A great silence surrounded us on this modestly large glade, with a forest of young trees facing us on one

side, which the Germans planted to mask the traces of the past presence of this notorious extermination camp. There was also evidence of a deep old quarry, which apparently was first used for hard labor and eventually for mass burial ground. The fading light, the solitude, the absolute silence, created a ghostly scene. The irony of it all was, that it all looked so pristine, so quiet without a trace of suspicion of what horrors were endured there by so many innocents men, women and children. On leaving, we have stopped at a simple cottage, just outside the camp. The local peasants, when questioned about the history of the camp, completely deigned any awareness of what occurred there during the war years.

When I became aware where my parents were found and taken to the local jail, I had a deep sense of foreboding that I will never meet them again, but an unexpected opportunity presented itself to see them for one last time. The remaining members of the Juden Rhat (members of the Jewish Board) a small contingent if the Jewish police and a few of the young men, including myself, who for some inexplicable reason were not included in the last round up, were allowed to remain. The Police were give permission by the Germans, to bring some food and water to the imprisoned group before they were to leave. I begged the commander of the Jewish police, who was a lifelong friend of my family, to allow me to be one of the carriers of the food, to which he responded with a sharp slap to my face and refused any help. I have somehow managed in this chaotic situation to be included in detail, which brought the food to the local jail, and to my great relief, I had the opportunity to be with my Parents for the last time. My intention, however, was to remain with them, which they would absolutely refused to consider, in case there was a chance for my survival. It was then in an effort to console me, that my Mother described our plight, as a cataclysmic event without any rational cause or reason. It was the very first time that I became aware of the word and its meaning. It was also, then and there that I committed myself to survive at all costs, so as to be able to tell it all and hopefully to reunite with my brothers. I was given money, a large gold broche with diamonds, in the shape of new moon with a single diamond star, facing it. It closely resembled the Turkish national emblem. It was my mother's favorite piece of jewelry and quite valuable. As it happed with out it and the money, as you will see later, I would not have been able to survive. This was a shattering event for us to be parting like this, with deep foreboding that we might never see each other again. I am convinced, that

it was it was at that critical moment in time that I, feeling a deep sense of anger ,changed from a dependent child, into a self- reliant sixteen year old man. Before leaving the prison I hid the broach in the bandages surrounding a suppurating sore just below my right knee. That they would allow us to return to the Ghetto from the prison was one the implausible decisions that the Germans would occasionally make. I left my parents shattered and bewildered, despairing about their fate. Feeling suddenly all alone, facing such an uncertain future and numbed by the events of the past few weeks, paradoxically I shed any farther fear.

Postscript

An unusual event occurred just a day after writing about the sad events above, which finally lead to the elimination of the Jewish population from Radomsko. I was visibly reminded of my very life there, by an incredible coincidence of unexpectedly finding and recognizing a bentwood chair made there before the war. Mitzi invited Lorri and me to have lunch at the "Renaissance" a small French patisserie, in Larchmont. Before sitting down at a table I noticed the unusual old chairs. I have alluded before, that Radomsko although being a small town had a thriving furniture industry. Such bistro chairs were manufactured there for worldwide export. Moreover, it was my fathers business that had the exclusive distribution rights for the necessary screws and bolts. I boldly announced to the two of them, that these chairs were made in my little town probably even before the war. To prove my contention I turned the chair upside down be to the consternation of the waitress who was about to call the manager. And there it was, a tattered yellowed label with the words, "Made in Radomsko, Poland." It might have also been likely that a member of my family and even I might have held the very screws bolting the chair in our hands. This physical reminder of my childhood years in Radomsko some sixty-five years ago, coming so soon on the heels of my description of the destruction of the Ghetto there, with the deeply disturbing memories, shook me to the core. It was an emotional experience, which brought me mystically close to those times. I was curious, of course, how these chairs made their belated appearance in Larchmont. Apparently, they bought them second hand on the Bowery.

The Warsaw Debacle

I have no clear recollection at all of the last days the Ghetto, nor how with a handful of young men, I found myself working during the day hours, in a German motor pool. The nights were spent in a dilapidated old cottage near the center of the town. It was at the end of Przedborska Street, opposite an abandoned row of butchers' stalls, just behind the town square, abating the main Catholic Church. We lived there for some time, but for how long, I cannot recall. I have absolutely no memory of why or how we have got there, yet curiously enough, I was able to retain and recall subsequent events in great detail. There were none of the physical barriers that previously limited our movements. We had relative freedom, which meant paradoxically, that we had no direct supervision. To venture outside the place however, unescorted by either the Polish police or the Germans, risked arrest or shooting on the spot.

Nevertheless, being convinced that getting away from Radomsko, might be a possible chance for survival, I chose naively to travel to Warsaw; there to seek out my maternal uncles Zygmunt and Henry. When I have last heard of them, which must have been a long time before, they were supposed to have been in the Warsaw Ghetto. Why I have presumed that finding them offered a safe haven, I cannot explain. To compound my difficulties, I had no information how to locate them. Dressed in jodhpurs and my highly polished riding boots, made me look at a glance, more like a middle class young Pole than a Ghetto Jew.(theses boots with minor alteration were my prized possession and lasted till South Africa). Having discarded my yellow armband with a Star of David, I walked to the railway station without being apprehended. In all probability, this might have been in part due, to the lack of awareness by the local Christian population, that there were any more Jews left in Radomsko. Equally surprisingly buying a ticket also presented no obstacle. Although this was my first train journey, after three or more years of isolation, it left no lasting impression and it was surprisingly uneventful. I was not so lucky however once I arrived in Warsaw. After hailing a doroshka (horse driven cab), I was almost immediately apprehended by two teenage boys who were running along side the cab, shouting abuse and leaving no doubt, that they discovered a Jew. It was a fearful moment, but fortunately the cab driver who must have been

a decent man, sped way, without a backward glance at me or the two hooligans. It was a close call, as they almost reached the steps, in an effort to yank me out. I am quite certain that had they succeeded, they would not only beat me up, but expose me to the Germans or the Polish police, either for a reward or for spite. If discovered, it would have probably meant a swift end for me. I gave the driver the only address I remembered, which was that of the prewar apartment of uncle Zigmunt. Fortunately was it was outside the Ghetto walls. He dropped me there without any comment. Having just survived a very close call, I got cold feet and decided then and there, to abandon this naively Quixotic plan to enter the Warsaw Ghetto even tough I was oblivious of course, to the terrible conditions there. I decided to return to Radomsko where I was more familiar with the surroundings, what ever the difficulties I might encounter on my return I recall wandering aimlessly around in the mean time, in the early autumn evening when I entered a pub full of light, warmth and happy noise, yet my own mood was one of despair and hopelessness, feeling dejected and foolish for deciding to come Warsaw at all. This particular memory was deeply anchored by the sounds of a boisterous "Skaters Polka" emanating from phonograph in the corner of the pub. I left almost immediately, with out waiting to be served, despite being cold and hungry, for fear of being recognized by some drunken lout. Later in life, whenever I would incidentally hear the sounds of that Polka, it would invariably provoke a sharp recall the outer sense of hopelessness and despair, as if it were yesterday.

Warsaw, by then was a city already partially destroyed by the by the German attacks, from the air and by the ground battles, of the 1939 invasion. Through out the city were scattered ruins of homes and buildings. I had no trouble finding even in the dim light of a street light, a demolished house with partially standing wall, behind which, well hidden, I hollowed out space amid the fallen bricks and rubble. I spent a cold restless night feeling every brick under my ribs. All I had for a cover was a light raincoat. The sleep has eluded me not only because of the attar physical discomfort, but more by the deep anxiety of might await me tomorrow. The following day, covered by an early October frost I made sure to shake off any debris of my clothing, but could not wash. Somehow, I found myself back at the main railway station and returned to Radomsko undiscovered. I rejoined the same small band of men, which I left only two days before.

GERMANY

How I Got There

After the return from my debacle in Warsaw, I resumed the work at the German motor pool or compound. Strangely enough, for the first time since the formation of the Ghetto, we worked side by side and even socialized with a group of young Christian Poles. Until then, with the progression of the German occupation of Poland, any contact became more difficult because of the rigid physical and social separation imposed by the Nazi laws. Until the dissolution of the Ghetto, any interaction between the Jews and the Christians was illegal, if it occurred at all unless it was sanctioned by the authorities or people took chances with their lives. While working there one day, I had a strange experience or may be an epiphany, but at a minimum, there were a series of coincidences that affected me deeply. At our lunch break I was joined by a young Pole, who during a chat showed me a colored postcard which he just received from a friend in Germany. This postcard was from a friend who was there as a conscripted foreign "slave" worker. It was sent from some place in Bavaria showing a lake at the southern end of which were the foothills of the Alps with gradually rising range of mountains crowned by snowy peaks. On the proximal eastern shore of the lake was either a church or a monastery. I relate this in detail, as it will attest to a strangely parallel event that happened two years later, when to my astonishment this vision actually materialized. I will recall this strange but seminal event later in this memoir. While holding the postcard in my hand, I was suddenly overwhelmed by an intense, though utterly unrealistic, wish to be there. I was also keenly aware that Switzerland lay just across those mountains. I had a fleeting thought that if by some miracle I could only mange get there, I might have a chance for an escape across the Alps to Switzerland; to freedom and life. Little did I know, that were I even to succeed against all odds, the Swiss were committed to return all escapees back to Germany, which apparently they did with great alacrity. In my circumstances such thought of escape were hardly even a pipedream. Nevertheless, for a fleeting moment a dream it was. Not a day later, when we returned from work to the old cottage, I was approached with a proposition by Abramowicz, one of the guys in our group; one of the few who survived the last action. He was one of those resourceful people who seem to thrive and prosper despite

adversity. Apparently, he was offered the working papers and an identity of a local Pole, who as a conscripted foreign worker in Germany, decided not go back. Abramowicz, who was older than I and somewhat protective of me, felt that this might be an unusual opportunity for me, as he had made other plans for himself. He suggested that I should consider buying these papers, as a possible way out of this hell. Now comes the strange part, in that these papers would allow the bearer to travel to Munich, the capital of Bavaria. At that time, Germany was a relatively large country, divided into many different provinces. That I might have chance of going of all places, specifically to Bavaria, was hardly believable. I was flabbergasted by the coincidence of my experience, just hours earlier that day when I so fervently wished to be there. The next thing I knew, we were negotiating how to pay for these documents. The sum requested was substantial and I did not have enough ready cash. My last resort was the diamond broach given to me by mother. I offered one of the diamonds in payment, but on seeing the broach, Abramowicz wanted it all. I had bargained him down to a single diamond and some cash. It was, however the largest gem in the broach, the one within the star setting facing the quarter moon. Thus I was still left with the gold broach, studded with the remaining smaller diamonds. That was a lucky decision not to fall pray to his greed, as this broach came to my rescue later, one more time.

The man, whose papers I had obtained, worked in an industrial complex of the BMW or The Bavarian Motor Works in Passing, a suburb Munich. It was there where I was supposed to travel in his stead. Very fortunately, he felt responsible enough to give me essential instructions, how to explain to his former fellow workers why I got there instead of him, if I ever were to arrive there. The story line which I was to offer them was that I as a Christian Pole, was actively involved in the anti-German political movement, had to leave Radomsko urgently, for the fear of imminent arrest. He also urged me to explain to them, that his failure to return was a sacrifice for the cause. The cause being my presumed anti-German activities in the Underground and that I was in need of escape. He further added that he planned to go into hiding to convince the local authorities in his hometown that in fact he returned to Germany from his furlough. Most importantly, he advised me that on my arrival there, I must immediately seek out a man called Stefan, who was the unofficial leader in this particular barrack. This proved to be an invaluable lead. The man whose identity I was to

assume was quite a bit older than I was at the time. I had to therefore, not only change my name but also raise my age by six years to twenty-two. I took my brother Bobs' year of birth and Ludwiks' day and month. This not only helped me to remember the dates, but I hoped to remain in some symbolic contact with them. At the time, I was barely sixteen years old. My major concern was how to be able to present myself not only to the Germans, but in particular what persona I must assume in front of my future Polish contacts. My serious anxiety was that on getting there, they might not believe my cover story but more over I might be readily unmasked as Polish Jew. The experience of the past clearly showed, that Christian Poles, like the Polish Jews could easily identify each other's ethnic background by physiognomy, manners or pattern of speech. It was fortunate that I spoke an unaccented Polish. Similarly, it proved extremely lucky that I never learned Yiddish, which might have left me with an accent. The similarities of Yiddish to German are so great that later on I might have easily confused the two at my peril. To fit my new persona, I changed my name to Malecki (pronounced Mauwezki) which in fact was a similar sounding translation of Kleiner from German to Polish. As it happened, it also happened to be the name of my father's business friend; a fairly common polish name. But until such time that I reach my destination, I had to travel under the name of Kowalski, the man whom I was supposed to impersonate. The papers, which I obtained, consisted of the personal data such as name, date of birth etc, but in particular, it stated that the bearer was allowed to travel back to his mandatory employment at BMW. It spelled in the details of such minutia as to give the number and the location of the specific barrack in the compound. Fortunately, it did not require photo identification. It was surprising to me that in the pedantic German officialdom culture ,one would find such an obvious omission in security. It was particularly so when security paranoia reached such heights during the war. I was very concerned also about the potential problems which might arise while crossing the border between occupied Poland and Germany. Again strangely enough, these worries proved groundless.

The next evening before I could get cold feet, I packed the few belongings I had left into an old battered suitcase. There was still danger that I might be recognized or accosted on the way to the railroad station, yet once again, I reached it without any untoward incidence and boarded a train for Munich. The train journey into Germany provided time for some

reflection on the rapidly moving developments of the past few days. The separation from my parents under these most traumatic circumstances, coupled with a sense of foreboding, that I shall never see them again, affected me deeply. Perversely, I also felt a sense of exhilaration to be free to travel, to be at last outside the confines of the Ghetto, after the years of a Gulag like existence, no matter how illusionary or fleeting it might all prove to be. Yet I was at the same time full of anxiety, as what to expect next. These moods alternated with a sense of bravado. The fear of the future, if any, was mitigated by my belief that to wait was to die. Therefore, the course I undertook could not be worse than what might await me. I vividly recall being enveloped by an alternating mood of an emotional void. As the train was passing the orderly German countryside, with the little neat houses with their red tiled roofs and small gardens, I reflected on the tragic fate of the Jews. In these times being one, was worse than the fate of a stray dog with nowhere to go. I considered the chance to leave for Germany an answer to a prayer, no matter how quixotic it might have been at the time. I have also rationalized that by going there, being so to say in the lions' mouth, might be safer than awaiting the inevitable fate in I were to remain in Radomsko.

I shared the train compartment, which I chose randomly, with a group of soldiers returning from the Eastern front. They were part of the Spanish Condor Legion named in honor of the infamous German Air squadron, fighting on Franco's side in the Spanish civil war. Now in return, they were fighting along the Germans against communist Russia. They spoke some German, but at that time, I also only had a very rudimentary knowledge of the language. The little that I learned in the one year at the gymnasium left me with minimal skills. I did, however, remember some German poetry. In an effort to communicate with the Spaniards or maybe trying to impress them, I foolishly recited the "Lorelei" by Heinrich Heine, the German poet , who because of his Jewish background was forbidden to be read. Fortunately, the Spaniards were either ignorant or unimpressed. Another unnecessary frightening incident occurred on the train, when on the way to the toilet, I found to my horror that I failed to dispose of my yellow armband with the Star of David. I found it unexpectedly it in my coat pocket. What might have happened if I were to be searched at the border? I promptly threw it out of the window when the train corridor was empty.

Munich and BMW

I arrived at the Munich Haupt Banhoff (the main train station) well after midnight. Incongruously my first act there, was to buy a pint of the local beer, as I heard that the Bavarians were supposed to brew the best in the world. As the public transport was not available so early, I proceeded by foot to the BMW compound in Passing, an industrial suburb of Munich. I suppose I must have asked for directions, as I eventually got there after what seemed like a very long walk. I arrived there just at the change of a shift, as I saw workers streaming out of the factory gates. They all were Germans, very few if any were young. To my surprise, they readily responded to my inquiries for the directions to the Polish barracks. It is interesting, in retrospect, how quickly I shad my fear of approaching any Germans, when hitherto in any personal contact with them previously in Poland, I was met only with distain, derision or brutality. I walked along the perimeter of the BMW factory compound, following their directions to the Polish quarters, where the foreign workers were housed according to their nationality. I became very impatient to get there. By then I was fatigued, not having slept a wink the whole night. I was also in a heightened emotional state, having undertaken such a journey into a hostile unknown, after so many years of forced isolation. I walked for some time without seeing any entrance gate, but only the seemingly endless tall chain linked fences toped with barbed wire which surrounded rows of barracks behind them. I assumed that these were housing units for the workers. Here again, I committed another of the many naïve, silly blunders which could easily have led to a crisis. Stopping in front of the fence, I threw the suitcase over the top and then with considerable effort I managed somehow to climb up the metal chain linked fence. Eventually, with great difficulty I was able to swing across the barbed wire at the top and jumped on to the other side of the fence. Not a moment later I was surrounded by several armed guards with drown guns, as instead of finding the Polish barracks I landed in the middle of the camp for the Russian prisoners of war. They too, were part of the work force of the BMW, but in contrast to the other nationalities, they were under strict military supervision. I do not know how I had the presence of mind not to panic but somehow I was able to explain that I was back from my furlough and by mistake, I landed there, trying to take a short cut. The traveling documents I carried, fortunately had clearly spelled details of my barrack's location. Instead of getting

suspicious of my unexpected presence there, they called up the central office. They must have had Kowlski's (the man under whose name I traveled) records there, which confirmed my flimsy explanation, as they took me to the gate and even gave me directions how to find my way. It is still amazing to me to this day, that they did not realize how unlikely my explanation was at the time. As a returning worker, I should have know better then to find myself in the midst of the Russian prisoner of war camp.

I have no recall how I found the Polish quarters, but I clearly remember the anxiety with which I awaited meeting Stefan, the unofficial leader of the barrack. I could not be certain as to my welcome, under these circumstances, especially as I suspected that he did not receive any prior communications regarding my potential or unexpected arrival, instead of his former co-worker Kowalski. I spent an anxious day until Stefan arrived later that day, having finished his shift in the factory. He was older than the other men, probably in his early thirties. He was easy to talk to and he put me at ease. I felt that he accepted the version of my political background and the reasons for the subterfuge. He intimated that he would try to help get some legitimate identification, also possibly a job position for me. In the interim, he told me that I could squat there for a time. I cannot exactly estimate how long I remained there in this peripherally communal way of existence, but life moved for a time into a regular routine. I slept in the beds of those men who they were working the night shift. I often had to switch from one bed to another, as they came from different shifts. Food was more of a problem. Not infrequently, some of the guys would bring me the remains of their meals. At other times I would venture, at some risk, to the workers' cafeteria trying to spot a plate with any scraps of food, before it was discarded in the garbage bin. I could not stand in line for meals like the rest, as I lacked the proper identification. Stefan thought that it was too risky simply to take the place of Marian Kowalski, under whose identity I traveled. I could not simply replace him, as I lacked any experience or had any of the essential basic skills to work in the factory. Nor could I take a chance to be recognized as an imposter by the German supervisors, who might remember him.

On occasion, I would venture with Stefan or others for an outing to the city, which was exciting. It was also a novel experience for me to be in such an interesting metropolitan city.

That my newly made friends did not recognize me as a Jew remains an unsolved wonder to me. It was perhaps that I spoke an unaccented pure Polish. My outfit of riding breeches and highly polished, expensive riding high boots may have given me some aura of belonging to the Polish upper classes, with some political baggage. I obviously belonged to a different social stratum than the rest of these young workers. I am certain that being under Stefan's protection was most probably the critical factor for my relative immunity to suspicion. In early January of 1943, I was still footloose with plenty time on my hands so to learn German, I would listen assiduously to the radio or read the local or national newspapers. An important paper at the time was the Bayerishe Beobachter (Baverian Observer) which was the main organ of the Nazi party. One day I noticed a small paragraph buried in the middle of the newspaper that the German High Command released the news of the strategic retreats from Stalingrad in Russia and from Tobruk, in northern Africa. I was struck by this news, as hitherto they never admitted to any reversal in the fortunes of war. Indeed, until then, the Allies whether the Russians, British or Americans were always on the loosing side. Germans, then the Japanese, enjoyed seemingly an endless string of victories in the early years of war; the Italians were the only exception having been ignominiously defeated in Greece. That evening, with much conviction, I told my friends "this is the beginning of the end" for Germany. I am very proud of my perception at that time, even though it was probably more intuitive than informed. As it turned out later, these two battles were pivotal in reversing the fortunes of war, in favor of the Allies.

As time went on, my existence in limbo was getting progressively untenable. Stefan was unable to procure readily, any new identification papers for me, which might have facilitated obtaining work, thus legitimizing my continued presence in Germany. He felt that my illegal presence in the BMW compound would eventually expose them and me to serious danger. He felt that based on his experience, I should go to the special police department in Munich which dealt with the affairs of those foreign workers who for some reason or other, lost their identification papers. I was to explain that I lost my papers on the way back from my furlough in Poland. By now, I too was seriously worried by the lack of progress being unable to settle. I accepted that I cannot remain under their roof for much longer. I finally resigned myself to act on, what seemed to me was a very desperate plan. To make sure that I

proceeded accordingly, Stefan accompanied me to the gates of the police headquarters, which I entered with a profound foreboding, that I will not leave from there alive Apparently the routine procedure called for a temporary incarceration until the personal information which I was to provide, was verified by the German authorities in Radomsko. At best, it was a futile attempt, as no such personal records existed under the name Jerzy Malecki. I was hoping against hope that perhaps I might be confused for the other Maleckies in Radomsko. I was sent to a rather well appointed office, probably because it belonged to a senior official, who was in civilian clothing and whom I was about to face. After giving the basic falsified personal data, I was told to get undressed and my clothing was searched. This senior officer suddenly became furious, shouting at me, how I dared to waste his time. He assumed that the only reason I presented myself there claiming having lost identity papers, was that I did not like my current job and wanted another position. He fumed some more, calling me a lazy son of a bitch, ordered me to get dressed , not to waste his time, and to get the Hell out of his office. What apparently provoked this outburst was, finding my traveling papers under Marian's name while searching my clothing. He immediately presumed that I did not like my current job at BMW. He assumed that all I really aimed at, by changing my name to Malecki was to get a new identity so as to be able to obtain an easier type of work. What I still cannot fathom was that before leaving my barrack for the police station, I had emptied all my pockets of any possible incriminating contents, as instructed by Stefan. How these rather bulky papers remained in my coat pocket unnoticed by me is truly inexplicable. After pretending to be chagrined and truly sorry, I dressed hurriedly leaving the office with an indescribable relief. It was a sunny winter's day as I boarded the tram back to the compound at BMW. As I watched the dreaded building disappear in the distance, I was suddenly imbued by a sense of confidence for the future. It seemed to me, that I was actually looking at the world through rosecolored glasses. Having just survived this encounter with the dreaded S.D. or the "Siecherheit Dienst" (security service), an arm of the Gestapo and left unharmed the offices of one of the most dreaded Police in the world, gave me courage. I felt that I might survive after all, groundless though, such thoughts might have been at the time. I was uncertain however, what kind of a reception I will receive back in the barracks by Stefan and the men. I related the unlikely events of the morning, but I am not convinced that they quite believed me, that I inadvertently forgot Marians' travel papers in my pockets. Now it

became obvious that something else must be done for me to become legitimate. Once more Stefan came to my rescue. He offered to try again to obtain some other identification, which then might lead to obtaining a legal job. This was essential if I was to remain in Germany, which after all, was my primary quest. Within days he produced a rather tatty, two page passport of a recently deceased Polish woman, in which they erased her name and substituted the name Malecki. My photograph replaced hers and it was stamped with a faked simile of an official stamp. It was a very crude affair to say the least, which caused me to have serious doubts how convincing it will be to the official eyes. Stefan farther instructed me to present myself with these papers at the Munich's "Arbeits Amt" (employment department), where with luck I will be issued new identification and an assigned job. He directed me to a specific window were I was to present myself. All this however required money, apparently for a bribe for an official at that office. The only resource I still had was my mother's diamond broach, which once again came to my rescue. I was apprehensive to offer it as barter, in case it would throw a suspicion as to my background. Who else but the Jews would have diamonds! Also having to give it all away, would leave me without any recourse, if any future need should arise. Recognizing that this was an all or nothing chance, I parted with this piece of jewelry, which had such deep emotional meaning for me. As it turned out, the designated official after a quizzical perusal of my crude passport and a somewhat cursory look at me, proceeded to issue a current legitimate official German identification passport for foreign workers. My photograph stamped with the "Hacken Kreutz" the official state symbol, made it all legitimate beyond reproach. Having in my hands an indisputable official identification after all I have been through was a joy beyond description. I was assigned to a work was at the municipality of Planegg.

Comment

As I will now begin to describe my life in Planegg, where I spent the rest of the war until the liberation by the American Armed forces in May of 1945. I feel the need to share with you my reflections on the events that preceded this fortuitous outcome. Since my arrival in Munich, I was given this refuge in the barracks of the young Polish workers, conscripted without any choice, to work at BMW. I still wonder how I was tolerated for a considerable

time in circumstances that must have been risky, not only for me, but in equal measure for my hosts. After all, as a group of strangers, they could have little if any obligation to tolerate my illegal presence among them. These young Christian Poles, of modest economic background, different social class, tolerated my presence among them, with calm acceptance and good cheer. I am particularly puzzled that through these long weeks when I had no alternative but to sleep in their beds when they were at work or sponge on them for food, I never felt any resentment or faced rejection. The greatest enigma, however was, that if there was any doubt about my ethnic background, it had never surfaced. What was particularly puzzling was the reality that I even lacked Aryan features. In a society where ethnic divisions between the Slaves and the Semites were so sharply drawn, one could almost say that they were bred to recognize each other to a fine point, by their physiognomy, manners or pattern of speech. I am equally certain that that vast majority of both groups can recognize each other readily. I also suspect that being under Stefan's wing, I was probably considered a political patriot, suspected of anti German activities in my hometown. This might have given me a sufficient cover. All I can say, that whatever suspicion might have arisen as to my identity, I was shown kindness, given help by total strangers, who took risks on my behalf. I now wished of course that I kept the addresses of some of the men, but at that time my only concern was to wipe away any traces of my past. The one other comment I would like to make is that I suspect that the success in obtaining the false passport and the eventual work assignment at the Arbeits Amt, not through Stefan's efforts alone. I suspected that he had a contact with an organized self help group of some sophistication. At that time, I also had a vague impression that Stefan was the unofficial leader of the Polish workers and belonged to a much wider circle of representatives of the various nationalities, comprising the work force at BMW. Furthermore, I thought such a group might have had contacts with either corrupt German officials or anti Nazi sympathizers.

Planegg and the Bauers

It is now early February 05, when I once again attempt to continue writing this memoir. I am looking at the river at high tide, through the large window in the television room. The occasional ice float moves with the current of the river, while a gaggle of Canadian geese

have just landed nearby. The surrounding marsh is covered with freshly fallen snow. Such domestic peace and contentment makes me once again intensely aware of my troubled past. For some reason last night, as I was trying to fall asleep, I had a vivid recollection of my life in Planegg, so I hasten to write some of it down. When I arrived there, with my newly minted identification papers and a job assignment to the local municipality, Planegg was still a very small town, just south of Munich. It was situated on the main railway line, to the Bavarian Alps, only about an hour away. It was actually a very pleasant place, with tree-lined streets, middle class homes and a general aura of wellbeing. Some of the wealthy Munchners had their summer homes here. The town had one Catholic Church, one cinema, one or two pubs and a large inn, the Gasthaus zur Eiche. Another reason d'etre for Planegg, was the annual pilgrimage to a revered Catholic holy shrine, and a prominent tuberculosis sanitarium, both of which were situated in the nearby forest. On my arrival there, I was directed to the local Municiple building, where I presented my papers to the Mayor. He was a pleasant looking man wearing the light brown uniform of a high ranking functionary of the S.A.(Sturm Abteilung) , the storm troopers, who were the Hitler's bully boys in the early day of the Nazi Party. They became eventually responsible in part for the civil administration). On his left arm was a prominent red armband with the black "Hakencreutz" (sfastica) in its center. I was greeted with a raised arm Nazi salute and a hearty Heil Hitler, which to my self astonishment, I reflexly replied . I soon discovered that such greetings were de rigueur among officialdom and Nazi party members. Others, especially practicing Catholics and simple folk, would rather evoke God by using "Gruss Gott" in their salutations.

Once the usual formalities were completed, I was issued the essential coupons for food, tobacco and clothing. To my surprise, I was told that at this time they actually did not need additional employees for the "Gemeinde" of Planegg. This caused me some immediate anxiety, fearing that I might be sent back to Munich for another job assignment. As it turned out, the Mayor "Herr Burgomaster" Stadler, found another assignment for me. I was directed to work on an outlying small farm which belonged to a friend of his.. The owner, Mr..Bauer was a wealthy builder from Munich, who as it turned out, was probably a war profiteer having avoided army service. The farm, in fact, served primarily for storing and distribution of building materials,which at that time, were at high premium because of war shortages. The

so called farm was in a little village just north of Planegg. Besides the farm house, there was a substantial vegetable garden, a small fruit orchard, and the usual assortment of farm animals, such as a cow, chickens and lots of rabbits in cages. The property itself was within a village, abutting on one side of the road between Planegg and Munich, while at the other end it sat on the edge of a large forest. The farm was actually run by the father of Mr..Bauer's and his wife. He was a tall, swarthy, heavily built man, probably in his early sixties, with a peasant's shrewdness in his manner and was quite talkative. I found him somewhat primitive and occasionally threatening. His wife was a small woman, matching him in age but with an indifferent affect, bordering on meanness. At first I slept in the barn, but soon enough, as they got used to me, I was given a space in the farmhouse's attic. The regular meals, three times a day, were a great improvement on my previous experience, yet chronically inadequate for a growing boy working hard physically out in the fresh air. I could have eaten twice as much given the chance. I felt hungry most of the time. I finally found a partial solution, which was when I fed cold boiled potatoes to the rabbits. I would snitch some surreptitiously for myself. I kind of suspected that the Bauers were snacking, when I was not around. I must stress how lucky I actually was, to have found this type of employment. I could have easily been assigned to work in a factory or to labor on a farm in the fields or even been sent in to the coalmines. It was, however, especially fortuitous that I could avoid working and living among a large group of other foreign workers, some of whom might have been Polish, and hence court a possible unmasking, a fear which haunted me constantly. The work was rather hard, as I really was unaccustomed to strenuous physical labor all day long, six days a week. On reflection however, I did enjoy being outside in the fresh air. The neighboring fields and the forest, with their particular sounds and scent, were a great compensation, despite vagaries of the weather. When it was not possible to work in the yard outside, I moved into the large storage barn. I often worked by myself, occasionally directed by Bauer, while at other times, I was part of a part of a team. At the very beginning, my main task was to bring some order to the various building materials lying haphazard all around the yard. A particularly hard task was to heave the long heavy wooden planks, so as to arrange them in neat, tall stacks in such way as to allow for drying and to prevent warping. On many days, I had to do this rather hard chore all by myself. Sometimes, I was helped by Bauer and on occasion by a youngish German with a limited I.Q, which probably was the

reason why he was not drafted to the army. At the beginning, I would wake at night with severe cramping and pain in my calloused hands. But this too, soon passed and I was not only getting used to the work but developed a good set of muscles. I was able to lift heavy objects, sometimes as much as carrying a bag of cement on each shoulder, a weight of about two hundred pounds or roll wheel barrels with rocks, up a gradient. As time went by, I lived a structured daily life with the Bauers. I was even eating with them at their table. I was able to listen to the radio, read the daily papers and on Sundays I would accompany them to morning mass, at the village church. I liked hearing the sounds of the church bells drifting over the fields, and then slowly dying in the distance. I especially liked those bells announcing the Angelus prayers, in the late afternoon. Besides working with the building materials, I also helped with the usual farm chores of looking after the animals or turning over the steaming pile of manure. On Sundays, I would often venture all dressed up for the occasion, armed with a carefully saved slice of bread. It was a happy time for me, when I walked some two miles to Planegg by myself, along the country roads. I anticipated with such pleasure a pint of beer in the local pub with a slice of bread carefully saved for the occasion. Sometimes, I would go to the local cinema, which was a great treat, after so many years being denied this pleasure.

During school vacation, the son of the younger Mr. Bauer, who was closer to my actual age, came to stay with his grandparents. Occasionally for having nothing better to do, Johan Bauer would talk with me. By that time, my conversational German was good enough to speak it with ease. One Sunday, the older Bauers made him take me along to visit Munich, which we did on foot. I do not remember any details of what we did in the city; I do have a clear recall of some details of our conversation, on the long way back home. With the unbounded confidence and arrogance of a member of the "Hitler Jugend" (a national youth organization), he declared his life ambition: with final victory by the Third Reich, hegemony which would include not only Europe, but also the United States, he would strive to become, of all places, the Governor of New York. As irony would have it, although in a less exalted position, I have arrived here instead of him. I do however, must admit to a silly act on my part, which I regret to this day. I offer as an excuse my heightened emotional state at that time. It was the first evening after the liberation, when mingling with American soldiers,

among the happy group of freed foreign workers, I spotted to my surprise Johan. Instead of being magnanimous or even gloating, I approached an American telling him of Johan's unfulfilled political ambitions. The sense of revenge on any German was so strong at the time, that it made me oblivious to any fairness. Fortunately, nothing serious resulted from this petty denunciation.

While my life and work at the Bauers became more of a sustainable routine, I became very interested in the course of the war. I could keep abreast of the news because I had a ready access to the German press and the radio. It was still early 1943 and despite the announced reverses in Russia and Africa, the German propaganda machine stressed the enormous losses sustained by the allied Merchant Marine from the German U-boats. The crews of the convoys bringing the urgently required food and materiel to Great Britain and Russia have suffered not only great losses of life, but had to endure the challenges of the most foul climate, so characteristic of the Atlantic and the North Sea. Listening to the radio or reading the papers was very depressing at the time, although I never had any real doubt as to the outcome of the war. Late in the spring of that year, I had an interesting experience, which left a lasting impression. A detail of Russian prisoners of war was assigned to log trees in the local forest, under the supervision of the older Bauer. This group was comprised of officers only, though older than I, yet we soon became very friendly with one another. I had an easy access to them as I acted as a translator because of the similarity of our languages. It was also my duty to bring them food each day at lunchtime. It was no mean task; having to carry two milk cans full of soup across the fields, until I finally reached the forest. They were very appreciative when I would dole out a generous portion to each man. After the meal, to my great delight, they would sing patriotic hymns, songs from home, and lonesome ballads. It was a memorable experience lying on the forest floor, watching the pines sway above my head, listening to their singing reverberate through the forest. To this day, I can still recall some of these songs and melodies. Once when they were awaiting the transport back to the camp, I translated for them an item from a recent German newspaper. It was of particular interest to them, as it contained the news of the intention by the Soviets, to dissolve the Komitern. They were quite mystified by this news, but on reflection they doubted that this would ever materialize. The credo of the Komitern was the concept of world domination by the United

Workers of the World, as the words of their anthem, the "International" clearly proclaimed; a.k.a. of course, Russian hegemony (we had the foretaste of this in Eastern Europe for fifty years after the German defeat). They voiced immediate doubts as to the Soviet intentions, laughing it off as a mere blandishment to appease any future fears of America and England. I, however, got into hot water by reading the newspaper and giving them political news from their country. Fortunately, it all blew over without any further incident, although I was abraded severely by their German guards at the time.

My time at the Bauer farm was rapidly coming to a close, I do not recall in particular why I was allowed to leave their employment. Perhaps it was on the request of the Mayor, who needed a replacement for the towns' street sweeper. The only one left to do the job was finally conscripted in to the army, despite his ripe age. But what sticks in my mind, was a particularly revolting grievance, which fired my resentment. It was the little dog incident. The Bauers had a terrier like mutt, which suddenly vanished from the farmyard without any sign of curiosity or sense of loss on their part. It was not until the evening when at dinnertime, I was given an unusually large portion of meat. It had an unfamiliar and peculiar taste. I also noted to my surprise, that the Bauers, had not eaten any of it themselves. I became aware that they were watching me intently and then smirking at each other. I then became acutely aware, to my horror, that it was not the usual rabbit dish on my plate, but probably the remains of the poor dog. I did not finish dinner that evening. At the next opportunity, I have incorporated this grievance, among others, as I went to speak to the Mayor.

Gasthaus zur Eiche

I approached the Mayor having serious trepidation as to the outcome of my plea to leave the Bauers' employment. To my surprise, he not only heard me out, but also gave me a job as a street cleaner, gravedigger and a general factotum for the Plannegg Municipality. It just happened that the previous employee who held this job, was drafted finally into the army despite his ripe age. This could not have come at a better time for me. After the formalities were completed, he offered to help me find a place to live, which I gratefully accepted. He

took me to his home where the Mayor, Herr Stadler lived on the ground floor of a building of flats that shared a large yard with the inn Gasthaus zur Eiche, which in a free translation could mean the Inn under the Oak Trees. In fact, the yard which housed the beer garden was dominated by a large stand of tall chestnut trees. I was happy to hear that he would approach the innkeeper for a possible rental of a room for me in this establishment. I was really quite taken back that I as a foreign worker and a Slav, considered an Untermench or a lesser human being by the Germans, was shown such consideration by a high Nazi party official. This was the beginning of my close and generally happy association with the family Ruch, who were the owners of the inn. We developed a friendly relationship and some level of interdependence, which lasted to the day I left Germany. They agreed to rent me a room at an affordable cost provided I shared it with another person who lived there during the working week. The inn was housed in a long two story building with the Beer Stubbe (bar), which also served as a restaurant. It occupied the ground floor, with an adjacent large kitchen. The living quarters were on the first floor with a number of small rooms on either side of a long corridor at the end of which was the private apartments of the owners, Herr and Frau Ruch. The room I was to share was a small, narrow space with a comfortable bed on either side of a small night table . The window looked out on to the trees in the beer garden. We shared a common bathroom, but most importantly, I was to have my meals at the inn. I was truly overjoyed and very grateful for this arrangement which was most unusual under the circumstances of the time and place. I expect that they might have been glad to have an able-bodied young man under their roof who might be of help or to give a hand in the various chores around the inn. As the future will show, this in fact turned out to be the case.

The owners of the inn, Frau and Herr Ruch were a colorful couple who deserve a full description. As you might have noticed above, I placed Frau Ruch, before her husband that was not the convention at the time, as she was the dominant person in the household and the chatelaine of the inn. She and her sidekick Mary, about whom I'll speak later, were in their younger years prostitutes in the Alsace Loraine region during and after the First World War. Apparently, Frau Ruch managed to save enough money from those days to buy the inn in the thirties. She then married the impecunious Mr. Ruch, with a proviso, so the story goes, that if she ever catches him cavorting with a another woman either uglier or older than herself ,she

will shoot him without a second thought. And shoot him she did, right into his beer belly .He must have recovered well, because by the time I got there this story became an almost forgotten gossip.

Frau Ruch was an imposing, handsome woman for her age, with a personality to match and with still some traces of former beauty in her face. Difficult for me to say now, she might have been in her late fifties. She was a rather tall, somewhat large imposing woman, with a heavy gait and both legs bandaged high at all times, covering what was generally believed were chronic syphilitic soars. She was invariably accompanied by an enormous German Shepard, which would shadow her everywhere. Her manner was forthright, direct but fair and nobody disobeyed her. She impressed me as a very wise, clever woman, who readily earned the respect of others. She was extremely good to me and very protective in a matter of fact way. Herr Ruch in contrast, was a never do well in his earlier life, but found his niche as a tavern keeper. He was the classic picture of a typical Bavarian beer drinker with a belly to match, a round florid face with slightly bulging eye but with a genial personality most of the time. He was fond of the proverbial trio of the pleasures: wine, women and song. He would appear late on Sunday evenings after gallivanting with his pals in Munich with a vaguely blissful grin on his face and somewhat unsteady on his feet and a box of cigars in a net carrier gently swaying from his wrist. Needless to say, he was not always welcome with enthusiasm by Frau Ruch at such times. What has endeared him to me was that he would occasionally invite me to ride along side him in his sporty two wheel horse drawn carriage. At times, he would even let me hold the reigns. Occasionally, he asked me to give him a hand at slaughtering and dressing a pig.

The other significant member of the ménage was Maria, Frau Ruch's sidekick from the early days in Alsas Lorraine, who was in charge of the kitchen. She was a small, middle aged woman, who was almost as wide as she was tall and always wore the same simple shapeless black dress. Besides being a good restaurant cook, her claim to fame was that when she was drunk, she would jump on a tabletop and dance wildly. This was a flashback to her younger days when she was cavorting with the soldiers in World War I, no matter if they were the Germans or if they were eventually the victorious French. I never really trusted her. She had

a mean streak but also, I had a sense that being a life long friend and a confidant of Frau Ruch's, she might have been jealous of Frau Ruch's kindness to me.

Frau Ruch had four daughters, I believe each by a different man, whose paternity were neither recognized nor legally acknowledged. They in turn, each had similarly illegitimate children of their own, again by different fathers, without the benefit of marriage or any sustained paternal presence or acknowledgement. Yet they all seemed to lead fairly acceptable social life at a middle class level. It should be remembered that the Nazi policies encouraged procreation for the sake of the State. I have amused to see a woman wheeling proudly a pram with one arm and holding another small child in the other, while a string of her older children of various ages followed behind. An order of motherhood given by Hitler, proudly displayed on her ample chest.

From time to time, I did meet Frau Ruchs' grand children and socialized with them quite easily. Strangely enough, they were all girls. I developed a close personal relationship with her oldest grand daughter Erica, so I was accepted by the whole extended family. She was closer to my actual age at the time, as I was then only seventeen. It happened that Lisa, Frau Ruchs' oldest daughter, lived with her two girls just across the hall from me. That December of '43, she invited me to join her and her two girls to celebrate X-mass Eve at their small apartment from across my room. It was a modest but very hospitable celebration. There were only the four of us that evening, after which Erica and I became close friends. This was playing with fire, as any fraternization between German women and the foreign workers, especially the Slavs was strictly forbidden. For a time the Matriarch, Frau Ruch tolerated this relationship without any acknowledgement, but as time went by, provoked by the inevitable gossip, she forbade any farther contact between us. She was acutely aware of the significant danger to us both. She would remark cynically that she suspected it was not the Bible which we are reading upstairs together. As the mere admonition did not work, she sent Erica to work and live in another part of Plannegg. This too, eventually failed to keep us apart, so Erica was sent to live in Aachen, in northwest Germany. I met her once more, for a short time when she has returned to live in the Gasthaus at the end of the war. Many years later, when Edith and I visited Germany, where I presented a paper at an annual meeting of the

Obstetricians and Gynecologists of the American Armed Forces in Europe, I made a nostalgic trip to Plannegg. The Older Ruchs were long since gone. I found out from the neighbors, some of whom still remembered me, that Erica was living in Munich and they gave me her phone number. The next day Edith and I met with Erica for lunch at one of the infamous beer cellars in the Marien Platz, in the center of Munich. Like us, she was by then middle aged, married and had two children. I was slightly bemused to find out that her husband was Jewish, when there were so few Jews in Germany at that time. I was glad to have the opportunity to close the circle.

My life, as the only full time employee at the Gemeinde Plannegg, revolved primarily around keeping the streets clean, helping at the local cemetery and at times assisting a local handy man by the name of Herman. Unofficially however, I also became the general factotum for the Burgermeister; but about this later. My work as the street cleaner consisted of a daily sweeping of the town's main sidewalks and the drains. The streets were lined with deciduous trees, so leaves in the fall, were a major challenge. To this end, I had to learn how to handle the two large oxen, how to rig them to the collecting wagon which I found awkward at first. The sweeping required no great skills and soon enough I was handling the broom with ease. Being out on the streets daily, allowed me to be accepted by the locals, who eventually not only greeted me but frequently stopped to chatter, which made the day go by quickly. I liked Saturdays best. By mid-day, as soon as I could out span and clean the oxen, I would return to my quarters, wash up, change into my best suit of clothes, polish my riding boots and then I was off on a train to Munich. I got a great kick out of contrasting my early morning activities at the luxury of sitting at some of the elegant cafes of the city. I also enjoyed perversely, the exhilaration that I, as a haunted Jew, was enjoying the privileges of Munich, Das Haupstadt der Bewegung (the capital of the Nazi movement). I felt that I was leading a double life in spite of them and for spite of course. At times, I would visit art galleries and museums, on other occasions, especially if the weather was nice, I went to the local zoo or attended a band concert at the English Garden, Munich's renown park. That was still long before the allied air raids disrupted the relatively normal tenor of the civilian life in spite of the war. I cannot describe the enormity of the change that occurred in my life; a transformation from an existence in a Ghetto of a small Polish town to this sophisticated metropolis. Yet, not for a

single waking moment, was I not aware of the potential danger. The specter of my true identity being suddenly discovered haunted me to the very end of the war. The presence of this pervading, uninterrupted anxiety left a lasting effect on my psyche, not unlike that experienced by shell-shocked soldiers returning from battle.

The work at the cemetery was particularly hard during the wintertime. The topsoil was frozen so hard that the wooden handle of my pick broke in half, as the iron spike hit the ground. Once the frozen top crust was overcome, the rest of the digging to the depth of six feet, was a breeze because the deeper ground consisted of very loose gravel. I was also frequently required to assist at burials. This consisted of getting into a black robe, helping to lower the coffin, and to my utter amazement, raising my arm in unison with the others in a Nazi salute followed by a hearty Heil Hitler instead of a prayer. I must admit, that the cemetery experience, left me with a perverse sense of satisfaction, for sending one more German to the grave.

At other times, I would have to assist Herman, the only remaining local handyman. Basically, he was doing bricklaying and carpentry for the municipality. He was also a drunkard and a home-span philosopher. Whenever I complained of the work being too hard, he would respond with a shake of his head and a retort, such as "if the work was easy then it would be done by the Burgermeister or the local priest". His other favorite admonition to me was "if the work is worth doing, then it is worth doing it well". This all was said with a wink and a smile. At first, he considered himself as the "Meister" and me as his apprentice. Eventually we became good buddies, eating together during work breaks or having a beer, to which he was devoted. The only work that I truly hated was the repair of chimneys. This meant that I climbed up a tall rickety ladder with a wooden contraption on my back loaded with bricks. With one hand, I held onto the rail while with the other I grasped the handle of the wooden carrier resting on my shoulder. I found this chore truly terrifying as the flimsy, tall ladder swayed more and more the higher I went. This heavy, unwieldy load on my back, made me feel that at any moment I could tilt inadvertently backwards, risking a likely fall. Somehow, I even survived this in one piece.

Like in most European countries, there was a very serious rationing of food and other staples in Germany. Each month the population was issued a booklet of rations 'stamps identifying the items, the amounts could not be exceeded. As I was eating at the Ruchs' establishment, I was obligated to hand in my ration card to them each month. I retained, however, the stamps for tobacco and clothing for myself. As I did not smoke at the time, these proved to be a very useful item for barter with the various merchants, as cigarettes were in great demand. Thus in addition to the food I was getting at the Gasthaus, I had ample opportunity to exchange the tobacco coupons regularly for an extra ration of sausage, margarine and cheese. It was a great boon for a perennially hungry adolescent working in the fresh air. Obtaining this extra food in exchange for my tobacco stamps or the actual cigarettes, became progressively easier as the Burgermeister began sending me to the various merchants for his supplies, which often far exceeded the allotted amounts. I also benefited from this largess. I was not only a trusted factotum to the mayor, but was regarded with some respect by the merchants. To this end, I was permitted the use of a small motorcycle which made me happy and proud, but almost killed me one time. When at first I tried to learn how to ride, I accelerated sharply up the steep driveway at the inns' yard, where by mistake I turned into an area strung with head high steel wire for drying the wash. It was only in the last moment that I avoided a probable decapitation by lowering my head on to the handlebars.

When I was working at the Bauers, they were occasionally visited by the local baker's daughter, who even then would allow me to buy bread without any stamps. When I moved permanently to the town, I renewed her acquaintance and for the rest of my time in Plannegg, I was able to buy every day except Sunday, a two pound loaf of bread and two delicious rolls. I stressed the latter, in contrast to the bread which became progressively more unappetizing, as the flour was mixed with potatoes among other ingredients, to add bulk. The rolls somehow escaped this fate. Caroline Steiger was probably in her early thirties when I knew her; a devout Catholic, with obvious antipathy to the Nazi dogma, as was the local Catholic priest. Curiously enough, on occasion, she talked of the good old times when she would voice her regrets about the fate of a Baron Hertzog, the former owner of a large estate in Plannegg. The Baron was dispossessed and banished by the government because he was a Jew. I liked and respected her very much, having been particularly grateful for her many

kindnesses to me. At such times, I often wondered if she sensed something about my background. I saw her again many years later, when on the same trip to Germany with Edith, we stayed overnight in her house. We still have a fine Meisen cup and saucer, which she gave us as a parting gift. By then she was already an elderly woman, but remembered me well and welcomed us warmly.

Anti Nazi sympathies were occasionally voiced in close circles of some Bavarians, I knew sometimes because they were devout Catholics, or by the Ruches who knew many of the high Nazi functionaries from their early days, most of whom had a very inconspicuous background. After all, the Nazi party paradoxically took root in Bavaria, despite the fact that Hitler was seen by the local Catholic Church as the Antichrist. It was also obvious, as the war was moved to a close and German defeat was inevitable, that more and more Germans became disenchanted with the regime.

My life at the inn took many forms. Starting with the all important food, I would usually eat breakfast and dinner in the kitchen, which was not only convenient, but noticing my enthusiasm for meals, Frau Ruch would sometimes give me an extra portion provided her side kick \Maria, was not around. On Saturdays, Sundays or Holydays, I would often help out by serving the food and in particular beer. I was shown by a waitress how to carry five large beer mugs in each hand, to serve the often boisterous customers in the beer. Another related chore was to roll up the heavy wooden beer barrel from the cellar, up the narrow stairs, place it up on a wooden stand and then with great care hammer in the bronze spigot. The next step was to avoid any extra spillage and prevent any excessive amounts of foam in the first few tankards. A particularly busy time was on the occasions of the pilgrimage to the holly shrine in the local woods. When once, after an especially heavy allied air raids, they released a higher quality beer with a stronger than usual alcoholic content. It almost caused a stampede at the inn. I remember not only serving it, but also drinking to excess like every body else. It seemed to me at the time, that it was a constant shuffle between the tables and the men's room.

Now might be perhaps the appropriate time to tell of a very strange experience bordering on the mystical. You might recall that my journey to Germany began with seeing a postcard from Bavaria showing a lake at the foothills of the Alps with snow peaked mountains and a cloister on the edge of the shore. This sight provoked such a desperate wish to be there, that when coincidently the same evening I was offered a chance to obtain false papers to travel to Germany and of all the places to Bavaria, I accepted immediately, although it might have been a harebrained scheme in the circumstances. The story, however, did not end then. Sometime in the spring of 1944, I was approached by Herr Ruch with a proposition to escort a horse to a friend of his, a farmer near the Stamberger See (lake). He offered a payment with a further inducement of a substantial lunch at the farmhouse. At any rate, I was keen for a little Sunday outing in the foothills of the Alps. He topped it all with advice not to miss at any cost, the beer brewed by the Monks in the nearby monastery, reputed to be the best in Bavaria. I guided the horse with some difficulty on to a railway freight car, where I tethered it securely. I then settled contently to observe through the wide open loading doors, the passing countryside on a beautiful spring day. The rest of this assignment proceeded uneventfully upon the delivery of horse I was paid the promised money. The lunch more than met my expectations. Remembering Herr Ruchs' admonition I proceeded to find the monastery. It took me a while to get there, as it was situated on the edge of the lake. With a tankard of brew in my hand, I went to drink it at leisure in the upper floors, which had views of t the lake and the mountains beyond. To my utter and complete astonishment, looking through the open window at the lake, seeing the Alps rising beyond, was a heart stopping sight for me. Incredulous as it might seem, it closely resembled the scene of the picture card, seen by me, on that fateful day in Radomsko, which set me dreaming when I so fervently wished to be in Bavaria. To this day, it still seams not only an improbable dream but a mystic coincidence.

Health and Friends

For most of my stay in Germany, my health, except for teeth, was remarkably stable. I experienced an occasional cold, but I have no recollection of any significant illness. If such were to occur, I might have been potentially in deep trouble, as I could not risk being

exposed to a physical exam, which might have uncovered that I was circumcised. As it was, when using the public lavatories, I always was very careful not to expose myself, by shielding in such manner as to not arouse suspicion .I deeply feared any potential visit to a doctor. There was a local physician whom I approached at all times with difference just in case I would ever need his services. Although he was relatively young, he appeared to be a reasonably humane and decent man, without any obvious Nazi fervor. Fortunately, there was no occasion to put him to a test. From time to time, I did develop severe lower back pain, which the Germans called a "Huxen Schuss" or a "witch's bolt", but I responded to rest and aspirin. My teeth however, caused me some trouble. I suspect that a prolonged period of poor nutrition and a lack of fresh fruit and vitamins might have been the reason. I had to endure and tolerate severe toothaches on a number of occasions, as I tried to avoid the local dentist who believed in extractions rather than treatment. Perhaps he was not motivated to give appropriate care to the foreign workers. The end the result was, that I accepted the inevitable fate, which was to allow him to pull out the offending tooth and he did without any anesthesia. I must say that it was an experience that I would not recommend to any one. Another unpleasant and rather anxiety provoking situation, was the time when I was stung by a bee on the lower lip. That gave me the characteristically Semitic look typical of the caricature in "Der Sturmer", the most vituperate of the Nazi publications portraying Jews with beaked noses and a thick overhanging lower lip. So I tried to keep out of the public eye for the rest of the day. You may wonder how one is bitten on the lip without having first noticed the bee. At the time, I happened to be working near an orchard, when I saw a pear tree with some ripen fruit. I could not resist snitching a low hanging pear, but not wanting to be caught, I bit into it with great haste. It was then, that I suddenly felt a searing pain in my lower lip, which proceeded rapidly to swell to an out size shape. I became quite alarmed, when I first looked into the mirror. Over time, especially on my frequent visits to the cinema, I became gradually aware that I might have some problem with distant vision. Once again, I worried that wearing glasses might give me a more Semitic look, so I avoided getting spectacles until the war ended.

I became more confident, particularly because of my close association with the mayor, I had enough courage to make friends with a small group of the only other Polish workers in town.

I became especially friendly with two brothers by the name of Dancinger. Clearly not a typical Polish name, which could have either been of German or Jewish origin. They worked and lived on the premises of the Baron Herzog's estate. We would occasionally spend Sundays together, one of which was quite memorable. They invited me to join a group of young men for lunch, where a freshly roasted rabbit was served. Unfortunally, they also provided a drink made from denaturated alcohol. It was as strong as it was awful to taste. Why we drank this dangerous poison, and poison it was, could be attributed to either youthful folly or a foolish bravado. I kept in contact with them for a short time after the war. When I was in London, I received a letter with a photograph of the younger Dancinger next to a grave of his older brother. They had returned to Poland, where as irony would have it, he died in an accident, having survived the war. The only other Polish workers I met later in Plannegg were two women, also older then I, about whom I had an instant suspicion that they in fact might be Jewish. They worked as domestics and each had older German soldiers as lovers. After the initial cautious feelers, we were glad to find each other and recognized kindred souls. We maintained a careful and only occasional contact with each other, but I become more at ease especially with the one woman named Zosia. It is she, who later after the war unbeknown to me, facilitated the first contact with my brother Bob.

Bombs and Wine

I learned to drink and like wine in most unlikely circumstances. Until then, beer or an occasional shot of Schnaps, the German equivalent of Vodka, were the only alcoholic drinks available to me. As the allied air raids started in earnest over Baveria, the Ruch household was forced to seek shelter in the relatively small wine cellar, which was surprisingly still amply stocked. Herr Ruch despite his obvious affinity for beer, which his belly clearly demonstrated, as a restaurateur in his bachelor days, developed taste for fine wine. To wit, there were bottles of Seck (German champagne), different red wines, but especially lots of Mosel, a white wine from the Rhein region. As soon as the sirens announcing potential air raid were sounded, we would all descend down the rickety stairs to the cellar. It was then that Herr Ruch, would proclaim with great conviction to me, as the only other male among the women and children, "Georg, we better drink the wine, before the bombs get it". I must

add that he echoed a similar exhortation at the end of the war, when there were still some bottles left, by saying "Georg, we better drink it all, before the Americans get wise to us". And drink it all we did. So much so, that soon the cellar was empty.

The Germans could not travel with ease at the beginning of the allied occupation. Herr Ruch, missing his wine, asked me if I would get a case of Mosel from his friends in Munich. I ended up carrying twelve bottles of wine on my back, in a large Rucksack (backpack) from the Marien Platz in the center of town ,to the railroad station and then into a crowded train. It was such an unwieldy weight and it required all my strength and effort to bring it home intact .I surprised myself that I was able to complete this task without breaking any bottles on the way. I was glad to be able to do him a favor, a minor recompense of all the kindness I was shown to me by the Ruchs. As a reward, I was given a bottle of Mosel, which I so clearly remember drinking all by myself, while sitting at the large window in the inn that evening, thinking of my brothers. I was so anxious for us to finally be together once more. The possibility that they may not even be alive had not even occurred to me, naïve that I was.

The air raids eventually become such frequent and potentially life threatening events that they deserve a more detailed retelling. At first, I delighted being the witness to the fear that the Germans exhibited. I shared with my friends and the other foreign workers this sense of partial revenge in seeing the destruction and panic which the raids were now causing the German civilian population. From the very beginning, Hitler, through the Goebel's propaganda machine, proclaimed a Total War, a euphemism for not sparing cities or the noncombatant civilian folk. But that was meant for only those whom they attacked, but were sore when the tables turned on the Germans. For some time already, we witnessed on a clear day the squadrons of B17 s flying over our heads at an altitude above the reach of anti aircraft flack, to bomb some distant targets. It was an inspiring sight to see literally hundreds of these bombers flying in perfect chevron formation, leaving behind their tell tale vapor trails, impervious at that altitude to any ground defenses. Surprisingly enough, I never noticed any German fighters engaging them in air battles. Eventually the air raids came closer and closer to us as Munich and its environs became the major targets for allied bombing.

If the raids were happening during the day, we could see and hear the bombers being shot at by the German 8,8 anti aircraft guns. The sky was full with puffs of black smoke in the vicinity of the planes, as the shells exploded near by, occasionally finding a target. I would sadly witness a disabled B17 or a Flying Fortress, the larger of the two, on fire and then disappear from my sight, trailing black smoke. On occasion, I actually saw the crew descending in parachutes. There was of course a lot of noise, both as the result of the sounds of the exploding bombs and the anti aircraft artillery. These air aids were not close enough at first to represent a life threat to us, or at least we thought so at the time. Soon after the sirens' alert was sounded, if no bombs were heard nearby, we would emerge from the cellar to scan the skies. One night, a raid over Munich was particularly dramatic. The sky was ablaze with light, the horizon was filled with a red and yellow glow from the resulting fires on the ground, while the bombers continued to drop the slowly descending multicolored illumination flairs to identify their targets. It all resembled a giant, shapeless multicolored Christmas tree. Adding to the chaos in the sky, were the ribbons of searchlights, which would occasionally find a plane in the cross of their beams. What one would see then, were the exploding shells around the aircraft, which would leave their ghostly image through a haze of gun powder. To compound it, was the din from the many anti aircraft guns and the sounds of bomb explosions in the distance. While feeling perversely a great exhilaration at that moment, I thought that if what I was witnessing was not an intimation of hell then I cannot imagine what else it might have been. (Only last night, as I was watching the Fourth of July fireworks, I thought that, perhaps these too, in many ways were reminiscent of that incredible sight, when the whole sky over Munich was like a huge film screen full of sounds, fury and blazing colors on the horizon.)

Eventually a day did come when Plannegg was singled out as a target for carpet bombing by the American Air Force. We knew that it was the Americans, as they usually bombed during the daylight hours, while the Brits preferred flying at the night. The term carpet bombing referred to a method when specific targets were not singled out, but instead the aim was to lay waste indiscriminately on larger geographic areas presumably of strategic importance. This of course resulted in much collateral damage. The two lead bombers known as the path finders, identified the periphery by flairs and the bombs were simply dropped in between the

designated area by their following squadrons. That particular morning, because the bombing began very soon after the siren warning, we must have sensed that this time we may not get of scot free. We were not even aware at that time of any specific strategic importance of Plannegg, other then the railway line next to the Gast Haus. Only after the raid was over, did we find out that the actual objective was the sub- terrainian oil storage facilities in the nearby forest. At the sound of first bombs falling, we found our selves in the little cellar with the mistaken belief that it would serve as an adequate bomb shelter, though I had my doubts. Huddled in a small space, we had to endure this time, a terrifying and seemingly endless air raid. By now, we were clearly aware of the serious danger facing us, as we heard the bombs dropping and felt the vibration of multiple explosions all around us. The terror of that moment was impossible to describe adequately. The eerie, whistle like sound of an approaching bomb, followed by a momentary stillness, heralded an explosion near by or direct hit. It was a heart stopping experience. There were so many thunderess explosions near by, which repeatedly shook the little cellar to its core. I feared that the very next bomb would fall on us, yet felt strangely resigned. When it was finally all over, hearing the blessed "all clear" sound of the sirens, we realized the miracle of our survival. The first thing, I noticed on getting outside, was Herr Ruchs' handsome horse running bewildered in circles in what remained of the beer garden. The tall chestnut trees, without exception, were all decapitated, not a leaf to be seen despite the late spring. The enormity of the damage was soon very apparent. The front wall of the Gast Haus, which was an elongated building, received a direct hit, so the Ruch's private apartment was destroyed. There were bomb craters along both sides of the building, some only a few meters from the stable, which bordered on the cellar. One other aspect of this unforgettable morning needs to be told. I have mentioned before that I was sharing the room at the inn with a civilian German, who for either health reasons or perhaps because of special skills, he avoided being drafted into the army. He boasted to me that morning that he had access to an especially safe bomb shelter, to which he was then rushing. On hearing the sirens' alert that fateful morning, I asked to let me go there with him, as I thought that I might be safer there than in our little cellar, but he flatly refused. As irony would have it, this seemingly safe deep beer cellar with reinforced walls which served as a bomb shelter for some select group, might have endured a direct hit,

but could not with stand the devastating blast of air created by an explosion, which ripped the door, causing a powerful downward draft of compressed air, killing all inside.

From then on, I never looked on of any subsequent air alerts as fun and games. I became totally terrified at the first sound of a siren. As soon as the alert was sounded, I would jump on my motorbike (a lesser cousin of a Vespa) and ride to the other side of town. Most of the time I would join my friends at the Baron Hertzig estate, where I stayed until the all clear was sounded. I was comforted by the thick stone walls of the eighteenth century buildings, but also because it was situated at the farther end of town away from the railway tracts. One morning as the sirens sounded again, I was rushing out in a panic, when I was begged by the Ruchs, Russian kitchen maid to let her ride with me. She, like every one else in town was terrified. So the two of us, the foreign slave workers were scooting out to safety, while the town's people, the Herren Volk had to run on foot to their shelters. Soon after the alert was over, I had to face a very angry Mayor, who demanded of me, if it was true what some people told him, about the two of us riding to safety on his motor bike. Either I must have given him an evasive answer, or I might have misunderstood him. He accused me of lying and he slapped me across the face. He also forbade any farther use of the motor bike. I was shocked and resentful by this turn of events. From then on, our contact became uncomfortably formal. Until then we had a most unlikely relationship of trust and mutual benefit, way out of the ordinary, when one considers the German attitude of superiority towards all others. In most cases, there was such a deep gulf with between Germans and the peoples of the defeated nations, especially the Slaves, whom they generally considered "Untermenschen" or lower human beings Overall I was treated so much better than most, but the complete answer why I was singled out, still eludes me. There was however a deep sense of irony in my situation, that not only was I a Pole, but a Jew to boot. Some of it might have been because of my attitude of trying to be generally helpful at all times. Over time as I became a general factotum to the Mayor. I earned his trust, especially after he used me as the conduit for the under table deals, with the various merchants. On other occasions I had to listen to him rhapsodizing on the virtues of the German culture. I was however, never invited for a meal in his home, though he lived nearby. Yet he trusted me to deliver a packet of important reports to the gathering of the Nazi bigwigs in Munich. I got a big kick out of it,

when I entered the smoked filled hall, full of men in brown uniforms with Swastikas on their armbands, the epitome of Nazism. If they only knew that some Jew were in their midst, improbable as it was then, at the time. The motorbike incident left me with bitterly disappointment in the Mayor, so much so, then on leaving Plannegg, I never said goodbye, nor to my regret have I acknowledged, his substantial help over time. The reason why I was treated so well by the Ruchs, having been was accepted by them almost as an equal, might have been due in part, by my ever ready willingness to help with various chores around the Inn, when such help was hard to get. In any way, it was out of the ordinary, how well I was treated by them and few others in this little town. I certainly have led a much better life, than was possible for most of the other forced labor workers in Germany. But what needs to be remembered, that not even for a moment could I afford to forget, who I was or why I was there. The fear of unmasking threw a constant shadow on my daily life.

Liberation Day

It is now early may 1945 and we were aware that we that the war is winding down. There were rumors that the Americans can be expected to be in Planegg any day now. It was a beautiful May day, the sky was blue, the sun was shining, the air was balm and could hardly contain my excitement. This long awaited moment has finally arrived, when I saw the first American enter the town. The overflowing emotions of this moment were indescribable and heart wrenching. The column was lead by a very tall Native American Indian (who could have come out straight from a Hollywood Casting office). He strode so proudly, looking neither to the left or to the right, followed by column of men in jeeps, with a single row of soldiers marching on either side. We were gathered in the eastern part of Planegg along the main road from Munich, leading south. By we, I meant to say that those who came to witness this long awaited historic moment, were mainly the foreign workers from around the area and some curious but apparently unafraid Germans. I was cherishing the moment, when suddenly we heard gunfire from near by and the whole street erupted in a pandemonium. I did not recall seeing any German soldiers for some time, so it all came as a nasty surprise, an unwelcome intrusion into an otherwise blissful day. There was of course an immediate response from the Americans and we all have scattered around for cover. An order was soon

restored when apparently the attacking Germans were killed. By noon, the town was fully occupied I believe, by the soldiers of the Seventh Army. That afternoon a private from the American command came to me with a request, to arrange for the burial of the few German soldiers who were killed during the unexpected scuffle earlier in the morning. It appeared that it was the Mayor who directed him to me. My first thought was to refuse this command, especially as it came at the suggestion of a former Nazi functionary, who I assumed was no longer in charge. Frankly, I resented this order, which I now as a liberated slave, should no longer have to do this job. I fought immediately better of it, as I did not want to antagonize the Americans. I do not remember how we understood each other, as my knowledge of English was limited to only three words. He probably spoke German. I agreed to organize a detail of men, provided they will allow me to gather some locals for the task. I also requested that I would need American soldiers to accompany me to provide the authority and protection. The cemetery was on the outskirts town and I was frankly anxious that there might be still some snipers lurking, in the woods nearby. I also decided that I might as well have some fun with it, so I chose only those Germans whom I knew of as committed members of the Nazi party. When we gathered them one by one, I told each that we are going to the cemetery but did not explain why. It was my first opportunity to extract some small vengeance for all the wrongs that the German Nation so grievously inflicted on others and especially the Jews. I wanted them to fear for their life, to get some taste of what the Germans did to so many others. Not until the graves were dug out, did they realize that it was not for them that the bells tolled.

In the early evening of the same day, I had an unpleasant experience with an American officer because of a misunderstanding that really upset me. He came into the inn with the request to find some accommodation for a group of men dressed only in striped pajamas, although I was unfamiliar with the concentration camp dress code I immediately recognized them as some kind of Jewish prisoners. I then whispered to Mr. Ruch that we must find some sleeping place for them, although there was no room at the inn. The American officer, who apparently was Jewish himself, must have overheard the word Juden (Jews) completely misunderstanding my intentions, hit me hard across the face. As I spoke Polish to the group, he immediately assumed that I was the typical Polish anti-Semite and was trying to influence

Mr..Ruch, not to help them when in fact the opposite was true. I was very indignant that I was so unfairly treated. When I explained the situation that in fact I am also a Jew, who survived the war with a false identification, he regretted his behavior and apologized at once. The evening ended harmoniously. The men were fed while I made bedding for them in the stable, on fresh straw with sheets and pillows. The next day they all left for Munich. It was amazing how the little town of Planegg changed overnight with the presence of a few hundred young Americans. First, I noticed they were surprisingly benevolent to ward the Germans. There was not even a trace of a conquering hero in their attitude toward the civilian population. It was so unlike the behavior of the ordinary German soldiers, when they were occupying Eastern Europe.

The most noticeable thing about the Americans was an overall pervading smell of coffee. It was on their uniforms, in their quarters, on the jeeps, even in the cigars which they so generously offered. In fact the whole town smelled of it. No real coffee was available throughout the war so this was a strangely new and a welcome aroma in the air. I was also amazed to see grown men throwing endlessly a small ball to each other with one hand, while wearing a huge leather glove to catch it with the other hand. What did I know of baseball then? Their other favorite pastime was chasing girls, of course. I made some friends among them, one whom was a man perhaps in his early thirties, who I understood worked as a music critic for a New York newspaper, perhaps even the Times. He too wanted to meet the Frauleins, so I introduced him to one who was a recent arrival in town. I was sure that she could not resist his charm, especially if it also included chocolate, cigarettes and coffee. I still have no recall how I communicated with them, but I spent a lot of time in the company of the soldiers. It is how I became a cigar and a cigarette smoker, learned to chew gum but not how to play baseball.

One evening I found myself among a mixed crowd of American soldiers, foreign workers and a few Germans gathered on the main square, when I spotted Johan Bauer, the grandson of the people on whose farm I worked when I first arrived to Planegg. It was the same boy, my age, whose ambition it was to become the Governor of N.Y. after the German victory assured the domination of the world, by the Third Reich for the next thousand years. If

nothing else, they truly never lacked boundless self-delusion and arrogance. I liked the boy, because he was quite nice to me under the circumstances, yet something triggered a resentment of that memory. I approached the one of the soldiers with that story, but I was glad on reflection, that the American either did not understand me or he just did not care. The program of denazification for young adults was not upper most on this soldier's mind on a lovely May evening. Almost immediately, I regretted this impulse to denounce Johan. Fortunately no harm was done, as he was not apprehended.

An observation that amused me no end was, how many of Germans who were the hard core members of the Nazi Party, removed from the lapel their jackets the NSDAP (National Socialist German Labor Party) pin and denied that they ever joined the party. The irony of it was that the pin with the Nazi Party logo, when worn over the years left a deeply embedded permanent depression on the lapel. This made a joke of the denial of their party affiliation in the past.

As soon as there was some semblance of order, I attempted to send letters to my Brother Bob in England, with the help the various humanitarian agencies. In the meantime I was still living at the Gasthaus getting along very well with the Ruchs. I became the representative of UNRA (United Nations Relief Agency) and the Red Cross for the Polish workers' community. This aid existed mostly for food distribution, to facilitate personal communications, such as letters home, finding relatives ect. I borrowed Mr..Ruch's fancy horse and buggy, to be able to reach as many as I could. I made a conscious decision not to leave Planegg until I heard from Bob. Looking back, I am amazed that I was so naïve to be confident that I will see my brothers again. I totally failed to take into account the contingencies of war. Little did I know how many perils they would face during that time.

A few weeks have past while I anxiously awaited some signals from Bob, when finally one early afternoon a young American private arrived at the Gast Haus inquiring if a George Kleiner Malecki still lived there. As he handed me the envelope, to my great joy I recognized Bob's hand writing at once. It is difficult to put to words my emotions at the time. The letter expressed his and Ludwik's great happiness at finding me alive and thriving as they were

convinced that I too perished in the Holocaust. More over he instructed me to wait until he personally comes to get me out.

Now, once more I must digress, to tell the story of an extraordinary act of compassion effort and persistence, how it came about that this young American soldier from NYC was able to find my brothers. You may recall that I mentioned that I met two women, whom I suspected were Jewish, who were living near Planegg in simillar circumstances to mine. After cautious feelers, we identified each other and became friendly enough to meet on a few occasions. They were a bit older than I, and one became especially friendly with me. Just toward the end of the war, a German officer came to stay for a few days at inn, while visiting his daughter; a soldier in the anti-aircraft defense group. He made a remark to the Ruchs, after taken notice of me that he was at loss to understand, why a strapping young fellow like me, speaking very good German and probably a Volksdeuch, (Poles of German origin) was not in the army at this critical time. When they informed him that in fact I was a Polish forced labor worker, therefore no subject to draft, he demurred long enough to appear to them that he became vaguely suspicious of me. When Frau Ruch made sure to inform me about this encounter, I became very nervous but of course I did not share my deeply felt anxiety with her. My readily aroused paranoia was enough for me to contemplate leaving Planegg at once. I became obsessed with the possibility that after all I that have lived through, I may yet not survive the war. The irony of having to face this, when the end was in sight, was especially galling.

The same day I sought out my friend, told her of my worries, and gave her the address of my brother Bob in England. I burned it my in to memory, at the time when I saw my parents for the last time. I was afraid of having an English address on me in writing, in case either I, or my belongings, were ever searched. The last contact with Bob six years before was in Birmingham where he resided at 1805 Great Lister Street with our Mother's relatives, by the name of Lesser. I have repetitively recited the full address to my self, so as, God forbid, not to forget it. It was for the first time that I ever have committed this address to a piece of paper's having asked my friend to please keep it, in case I should disappear from Planegg or was to die. In that event, I specifically asked her to write to my brothers to say that I have

tried to survive, even if I could not make it in the end. However, as suddenly as the perceived threat appeared, my problems resolved, as the German officer was suddenly recalled to his unit. I have again contacted my friend, this time tell her of the unexpected happy outcome. The war soon ended but I never had the opportunity to see her again.

What transpired, however, is that she became a girlfriend of the American soldier, who delivered Bob's letter to me. This young man, to whom I was a total stranger, was given Bob's address by her. He took it upon himself to travel under very difficult circumstances at the time, all the way from Munich to Birmingham, with the news of my survival. Not having found Bob there; he then continued to London, to my brothers' flat on Great Portland St. and waited on the staircase for four hours, until Bob got home. There was apparently great jubilation on hearing the news and Bob with his friends expressed their gratitude by giving him a good time, for the rest of his stay in London. There was no adequate compensation for his giving up a well-deserved furlough to make such great effort for a total stranger. I regret so much that I did not have the presence of mind at the time, to ask for his address in N.Y. What a privilege it would have been for me to have an opportunity to meet him again. But then again who could have known then, that I would be living in New York.

Bob managed eventually to locate Ludwik in Scotland, who received the joyful news in a state of shock and promptly left AWL (absent without leave) for London. Apparently, the news of my survival was celebrated long and well with their friends. Ludwik however paid for his enthusiasm and joy with a few days in jail on the return to the base, which he left without official permission, which was denied him at the time.

As I was awaiting farther communications from Bob, I became very friendly with another Polish boy, who lived nearby. His name was Jan Mikolajczyk, a nephew of then prime minister of newly formed Government of Poland. Early on, there was a pretense by the Communists in Warsaw and their overlords in Moscow, to include some political figures from the London government in exile. As Mikolajczyk was the chairman of the Peasant Party, the Communist government in a lip service to Western allies, appointed him to prime minister, only to be dismissed shortly after. Short time later he disappeared without a trace.

His nephew Jan hesitated to return home to Poland living in the mean time with a lovely girlfriend Zosia; a classic Polish beauty. She worked during the war as domestic for an important family in Planegg. She remained in their house after the war for a time being and was befriended by the two rather handsome daughters of the family. They lived in a sumptuous villa at the edge of the forest. I was invited there one evening to party with Zosia Jan and the two girls, whose parents were away for a few days. After dinner and a few drinks as we were dancing, there was, a knock on the door asking for me in name. To my great joy, before even the door even opened, I knew that it was Bob. Once again the emotions of the moment defy description. You can only imagine what a fantastically exciting night it has been, and not only for Bob and me, but also for the others who shared in our joy. In fact we never went to bed that night as the party continuing into the hours of the morning of the next day. Once we bid them all fond farewells Bob and I went back to the Gasthaus where I changed into the uniform of an R.A.F. (Royal Air Force) officer's uniform. We then went to say good byes to the baker's daughter, to the butcher who gave us a whole ham, and after thanking the Ruchs for all their kindness, we left for Munich and hence to Paris. Was I dreaming?

TO PARIS AND BEYOND

The 14th of July and Other Jinx

The train from Munich to Paris was cramped full of young men with an occasional female here and there. These were soldiers of many nations, but were predominantly comprised of Americans. There were some Poles in our compartment, so I could avoid having to explain why I could not speak English, while wearing a British uniform of an R.A.F. officer. I am not sure if we needed any tickets, nor do I have any memory, how we even got on to the train. The events of the previous twenty-four hours were so momentous and emotionally overwhelming for me. All I felt was only a deep sense of joy and relief, that after so many years, despite all adversity, I was finally reunited with Bob and will see Ludwik very soon. The realization that I am leaving Germany alive and in one piece and that of all the places, I will be going to Paris was difficult to absorb. My nineteenth birthday was just a few weeks before and I could not think of a more glorious birthday gift. The final objective, however, was to get me to England, where I was to join the Polish Army, as the war with Japan was still raging on.

Soon after arrival to Paris, we were invited by some friends of my brothers for dinner. I was glad to be able the contribute the large ham, given to me on my departure from Planegg. This was not a mean gift, as food was still a problem in Paris at that time. Despite the shortages, it was a classic French dinner, consisting of many courses. It was also then, that I had a slightly embarrassing moment, when after the dinner we all went in to the garden adjoining the house, when feeling a large bulge in my trousers, I pulled out a large dinner napkin from my pocket, to every body's amusement. Such refinements as dinner napkins, was not to what I was accustomed for the past few years.

The following day we went to the British Consulate, to obtain a visa for me to enter England. We were met with an absolute rejection despite, that my brother Bob was a highly decorated hero of the Polish air force under the British Command and I was a Holocaust survivor. All

our entireties were rejected out off hand. Bob then thought that perhaps, if I could join the Polish Army in France, that might possibly, get me eventually to Britain, where the bulk of the Polish Army in Exile congregated after the war with Germany. The following day I enlisted into the Polish army, which by now had only a small garrison in Paris. This uncertainty as to the outcome was a serious setback for us. The fact that Bob must be soon returning to his unit in England, was also causing some anxiety.

Yet in the meantime, there was Paris, physically untouched and ebullient in all its post- war euphoria. It was an early July, the days were sunny and warm, and I was literally like kid in a candy store. I was more than ready to explore and experience the longed imagined pleasures of this wonderful Town. Visits to Louvre, where I was free to look at the Mona Lisa eye to eye and on the eye level, unimpeded by either protective glass or height. I was photographed cuddling next to the statue of Venus de Milo, without having to worry about being warned off, by the museum guards to stand back. We visited the Palace of Versailles, where I heard the ungrateful French, cynically commenting on the generosity of Betty Hutton, the Woolworth millionaires, who donated monies for the restoration of the Hall of Mirrors, which was famous as the site final peace agreement of World War I. Then there were the grand boulevards, with its many sidewalk cafes and even at that time, delicious pastries. Watching the Parisian girls was of course obligatory. For as long as, Bob remained with me in Paris, I would regularly accompany him for lunch or dinner at the British Officers' casino where there was great food and Champagne, though to Bob's chagrin, I still craved beer. The casino was in a very elegant palace, which previously belonged to the Rothschilds.

One of the greatest memories of Paris, for me, was to be able to observe and participate in the festivities of the commemoration of the Bastille Day. Since end of the war, this was the first time when this important national Holiday was celebrated. On the evening of fourteenth, the first day of the celebrations, there were spectacular fireworks, which seemed to set the river Seine ablaze. It was so exiting to stand on one of the bridges or mingle with the enormous jubilant crowds. There was music, singing, and dancing on the streets, to the wee hours of the morning. I have met a pretty girl and somehow with the few paltry words of French, I

extracted a promise for date, for the next day, to which she eagerly agreed. She assured me that she would even bring her mamma along for the occasion, so regretfully I declined.

Bob was about to leave back for England as he was at the end of his furlough, when we heard the disquieting rumors that the French government was planning to disband the small remnants of the Polish army. But by far the worse news, was the threat, that once demobilized we would not be allowed to remain in France. This meant that we might have to return to Poland. It was only a day or two later, that we heard in the barracks, of a future recruitment effort for sailors, to beef up the Polish Navy in Great Britain. This was, however, restricted to only those with a previous maritime experience, preferably to those who already served in the Polish navy, before the war. Well, a good fortune once more smiled on me, by having met in the barracks a fellow soldier, former bosom, in the Polish Merchant Marine. His name was Marian and he was considerably older than I. Told of my desire to join my brothers in England, he encouraged me to try to enlist into the Navy Program. He suggested that I could pretend that I too served in the Merchant Marine before the war. He offered to tutor me in the basics of ship structure, sea culture and language. He also identified a specific schooner on which I was supposed to have served as a cabin boy to the Captain as I was too young to pretend otherwise. He gave me his name, as well as that, of the senior officers of the ship, all of which I was to memorize. Finally, I had to face a panel of five navy officers sitting across a table. After I saluted smartly, I was interviewed in detail about my supposed past experience in the navy. To my utter astonishment and great relief they have some how accepted my responses to their detailed questioning. I was then formally enlisted in the Polish Navy and was to be included in the next transport to England.

Bob and I celebrated with Marian my success well into the night and insisted that he accepts some money as a reward for his initiative and efforts. Only in retrospect did I realize that were I to have failed the interview, I might have been subject of a court marshal. Within days I was shipped out in a group with others, to Portsmouth in Southern England. We left from the port of La Havre, which still showed the scars of the intense fighting there during the Allied invasion. I was immensely grateful for how fortunate I was, to be able to enter Great Britain, so unexpectedly, despite such serious earlier obstacles. Even the notorious English

Channel was calm enough, to allow for a smooth sail. In my pocket, I had some English coins given to me by Bob, but spoke or understood hardly any of the language. It took me some while to speak it, but much longer to understand their monetary system of Guineas, Shillings Farthing and Pence. What joy it was to have finally reached the English shore; what's more in my own skin and with my own name.

England and Scotland

The fifteen months that I spent between England and Scotland made a great impact on me. It was a time of personal growth, full of rich and varying experiences, but nearly totally void of any formal schooling, which was interrupted by the war except to have learned colloquial English. I will try to describe those months during which I experienced a life at such a high level of intensity. On leaving England, but especially London, I was of a mind, that it should be obligatory for every Continental European to spend a year there, in order to become civilized.

We have arrived to Plymouth early in the morning and were immediately taken to the Polish naval base there. Soon after, we were greeted by the commander who, with a very stern demeanor, read out to us the riot act of behavior. He accentuated that this is the navy and not the army. He spelled out the rules of conduct and discipline, one among which was that smoking was restricted on the base, to certain hours only. I have sensed immediately that the Navy may not be for me, the ideal choice of service. At the next free moment, I called Ludwik, first to greet him after so many years of separation, and then related to him my anxiety about staying in the Navy. His response, after the years of experience dodging the army discipline, was the advice to apply immediately for a transfer to the army. It also helped that that he knew a commanding officer, who might help. When I faced the Commander of the base with my request, it was granted with some distain, but I was permitted to change the services. I was given transfer papers to an army base in Kinghorn in Scotland, just north of Edinburgh. We arranged with Ludwik that I should meet him on the way there, at the Euston Railway Station, in London. I could hardly wait for the moment, to see him again; as I am sure, he was as well. Yet it was not to be. There were such crowds on the platform, that we

have somehow missed each other. My inability to speak English did not help, but it was bitter disappointment at the time for me as I am sure it was for him. As soon as I have arrived at my destination I called him in London and again we have arranged to meet, but this time in Kinghorn where I was based. The travel during those times was rather complicated as first one had to obtain a leave from the army unit, then request a voucher for the train ticket, which for the armed forces personnel was cost free, but difficult to obtain. As a residue of the war restrictions each train had a slogan across its locomotive. "Is your journey really necessary?" This was especially true for the long distance intercity travel, such as between London and Edinburgh. As time went by these restrictions eased off. I had often had the opportunity to travel on a famous, fast train between these two cities called "The Flying Scotsman". Even then, there was a dinning car, where in particular, they served marvelous eggs and keepers, to which I am addicted to this day.

I will never forget the moment that Ludwik and I met on the moors Scotland. He called the previous day to give me the proximal time of his arrival. I was very anxious to be on time to greet him at the station, as we planed. The army barracks to which I was assigned was situated outside the little town of Kinghorn, on the top of a large hill, over grown with short brush and heather. When the hour of his expected arrival came near, I began the decent on the narrow pathway from the base to the little town, when I spotted a small, solitary figure way down at the bottom of the hill. In a blind conviction that I was my brother, I began to shout his name, as I run down. Simultaneously Ludwik noticing me did the same. Needless to say, it was a breathless, deeply emotional meeting for of us, after so many years of separation, upheavals and the unlikely chance the it would ever take place at all. The commanding officer was well acquainted with Ludwik, so I was assigned to the adjutant's office, which was plum job. I was also granted several weeks of compassionate leave to recuperate after my war experiences.

Thus began a short period of total indulgence being the guest of the Poseys in their country house by the sea. It was also the time for an intense effort to learn basic English. My brother Bob became very friendly during the war with a Mr. Posey, a wealthy businessman, who also originally came from Poland. He was a relatively small but a sturdy man, with a rather brisk

manner, who did not suffer fools gladly. Mrs. Posey in contrast was an attractive woman, who might have fitted the description of statuesque. She spoke English with a moderately thick Russian accent which, in a way, was quite charming. As I recall, Mr. Posey considered her as bird-brain, treating her with some degree of disrespect. They had two children, George who was my age and Edward who was two years younger than I. George unfortunately was significantly affected by cerebral palsy at birth, which left him with some neuromuscular defects of arm and leg on one side, which made him clumsy and unable to complete fine tasks. He also had some speech defect, so he drooled and sprayed saliva while talking. It also affected his intelligence to some degree, may be due to a lack of an early rehabilitation. He was quite sweet, however, always very grateful for any attention. His brother on the other hand, who was the apple in his father's eye, was an intensely energetic, smart boy. The Poseys had a cottage in Birtchington, on the coast, south of London. The boys and I were dispatched with Mrs. Posey and their maid, with the implicit instructions to fatten me up, which I hardly needed, as I was in a very good physical shape. Most importantly however, I was there to learn English. Although occasionally I would resort to broken Russian, to speak with Mrs. Posey to with translation, but we all endeavored to speak predominantly English. There was marvelous food and plenty of it, so much so, that I would often finish my deserts in an easy chair, being unable to sit at the table any more, after such over eating. It was at the many hotels at this seaside that I witnessed to my surprise, people dancing in the Conga line or in utter disbelieve I watch them do the Jitterbug. When I have seen these dances portrayed on German News Reels, I thought it was so crazy, that it had to be a fabrication of an anti-Allied propaganda.

The most astonishing and unforgettable event, which occurred during my stay there, was the special announcement on the radio, interrupting a regularly scheduled program. We were just finishing the lunch when the BBC radio announcer gave a news flash that, an enormously powerful, single bomb, corresponding to many thousand pounds of TNT, was dropped on one of the Japanese cities, causing untold damage. He also implied that it was a product of new technology that he called atomic energy. There were no discussions at that time about the long-term implications, nor that a new dramatic era, has just arisen.

I had a wonderful few weeks in the cottage and then the remainder of my furlough was spent in London. After an additional short course for foreigners offered by the London City Council, to learn English, I was able to understand and speak at a very basic level; after some six weeks in the country. I followed on my experience learning German, which was one of total immersion in the language. Such a discipline included lots of listening to the radio, simultaneously reading the newspapers, both which were readily available to me. Most importantly however, I was not afraid of making mistakes, even if it made me look foolish at times.

I was fortunate to be able to visit London frequently as I was actually, stationed in Scotland. I was based at first at a garrison in Kinghorn, a small town on the east coast, just north of Edinburgh. To travel there on the train, one had to cross a broad inlet, on a one of the most famous iron bridges of the world. The Forth Rail Bridge was a gigantic structure that as many time that I crossed it, never failed to impress me. Life at the army base was pleasant enough. It was there that I first tasted the ubiquitous Fish and Chips. Then, they were indeed still wrapped in old newspapers and sprinkled with the mandatory salt and vinegar. Very soon after my arrival in late summer, I noticed one Sunday, people swimming in the bay. The next day I went down to the little town and bought myself swim trunks planning to go bathing before the summer was out.. The last time I spent at the seaside was in Zoppoty, near Gdansk on the Baltic, when I was three years old. I only remember this from a photograph of our family posing on the pier. I often looked at it, which might have inspired a vague longing for the sea throughout my childhood. (I visited there again with Edith on our trip to Poland in 1988 and found the exact spot where the photo was taken). On the next warm day in Kinghorn, I went swimming. I run without thinking into the shallow waters of the little harbor, having seen people bathing farther in the sea. All of a sudden, as the water reached my chest I became aware of the intensely bitter cold, which overwhelmed my body, almost to a point of paralysis. The temperature of the North Sea was well below that which I could tolerate, never mind enjoy. As fast as I run in, the faster I run out and the swim trunks were never put to such use again.

Any weekend which I did not spent to London, I would visit the neighboring towns where I would invariably spent some time in the soldiers' Canteen, where food, drink and companionship was available.

The greatest fun though, was going to Edinburgh. The great Princes Street with its many shops and cafes and the huge castle hovering over it, from the hill, on the other side, was memorable. Especially enjoyable experience for me, were the four o'clock tea dances, at the various cafes. I improved my dancing skills and the Scottish lasses were charming. Such one trip got me in to a real trouble with the commanding officer of my base. As I was working in the regimental office, I was able to write weekend passes and issue rail tickets to London for myself. On one such weekend, when visiting London I got severe flue and could not get back in time. Despite presenting doctor's certificate I was declared A.W.L. (absent without leave). I was given a three days detention, in an improvised jail, which consisted for some reason, of a half a cellar in some building away from the base. I was quite miffed, feeling that it was unjust and had a valid excuse. In reality, the whole thing was a joke. My friend would bring me food and the guards would take me for a walk in town. On my return to the base, I was grounded. As the next weekend was soon after my return from jail, I thought that I deserved a break and in spite of the injunction not to leave the base, I took myself that Saturday afternoon to the local railway station. To my distinct discomfort, I noticed my commanding officer on the platform while he spotted me at the same moment. At first, I decided to abandon my plan, but as the train started to leave I jumped on to the steps of the last wagon hoping that I was not noticed. Half way through the journey, I got cold feet and left the train at the next stop. I hiked a lift only to discover that this nice Scot was going to Edinburgh, and not in the direction of Kinghorn. So once more, I had a change of mind and planned to enjoy my weekend in the big town, after all. I asked to be dropped far away from the railroad station, so as to avoid any chance of running into any one I knew. As luck would have it, as I turned the corner on to Princess Street, I run smack into my commanding officer. Chagrinned I saluted, he smiled and that was that. To my great surprise, there were no repercussions from this incidence. What I learned from it is however, that sometime one should not press one's luck in matters of no importance. Another memory of my life in Kinghorn, was the ever

present repetitive mournful sound of the fog horn reaching us high over the moors, from across the bay, which accentuated the sense of isolation and the occasional loneliness.

As long as I remained at the base in Kinghorn, I was able to visit London frequently. Working in the adjutant's office as a clerk, I could readily obtain both the weekend pas and the train ticket through the "generosity" of His Majesty's Government. Our life in London was quite outside the realms of the ordinary soldier. My brothers somehow had enough money to have spacious flat in the West End, on Great Portland Street, which runs from Oxford circus to the Regents Park. Bob also drove a small Austin. In those days, we would frequently go to restaurants, cinemas and often visit for dinner with the Poseys.

Through Ludwik and Bob I have come across many interesting people, these were in the main young, most of who were members of the arm forces, still in uniform. I was very pleased to have met Bob's navigator, whom my brother credited for having survived the fifty missions while they flew in combat together, over Germany and the occupied France. Of their whole squadron only a few came out alive or at best in one piece. The reason for such high attrition rate was not only due to the enemies' defenses, but also because of the very nature of the airplane itself. The Mosquito, which Bob flew, was a two engine fighter bomber, literally made out of plywood covered with canvas, but it powered by two disproportionably heavy engines. This made the Mosquito one of the fastest planes, until the development, of the jet engine late in the war. The disadvantage of a top-heavy airplane was that number of Mosquitoes was lost on takeoffs and landings. The English weather was, of course, a serious additional hazard. Bob was a man relatively short in stature, so to reach the controls of the plane he had to sit on a pillow. He was a feisty fellow, obviously very brave, who was awarded significant medals for his war efforts. He looked very handsome in his uniform of an Air Force officer, with the cap at a jaunty angle on his head. I was so proud to be walking along him.

Another person who comes to mind is a Dr. Kryszek and his wife, who befriended Ludwik. Apparently he was a friend of our father's from before the war. By the time, I have arrived in London this was a well-established relationship and I too benefited much from their

hospitality. This was a home in which many of the Polish émigrés intellectuals gathered for a good meal, followed by some very intense exchanges, which was a privilege to witness. It was there that I met the famous satirical Polish poet Tuwim.

Soon after I arrived to London, my brother Bob met Audrey Balleny, a niece of the owners of our flat in London. The flat belong to a Merchant Marine Captain and his sister a Miss Lee. As the Captain was away for extended tour of duty, it was Miss Lee with whom we were in frequent contact and thus he happened to meet Audrey, his future wife. Their meeting blossomed into romance and they became constant companions. Audrey at that time worked for the Bank of England, a venerable institution. I also became very fond of Miss Lee and would meet them on occasions. Many years later when Edith and I were in London, we went to visit her in Greenwich and enjoyed very much renewing our friendship.

There was one restaurant in London I found to be especially interesting. It served the traditional Polish food, as it was a part of the Polish club Called 'Ognisko", which when loosely translated means "Hearth". It was situated in Kightsbridge facing Hyde Park. The club was a gathering place for the Polish expatriates, the former members of the government in exile, the army brass, and some remnants of the Polish nobility, as well as some ordinary folk. For those of us who left Poland many years before, being there it was like watching a comedy of manners. What made it so comical were the pretentious mannerisms and social attitudes of the pre war years. Being addressed by the former title, be it of a ranking member of the armed forces no longer in existence or by the title of the long discounted noble family, was de rigueur, such as Pan General this or Pan Hrabia that (Sir General, Sir Baron). I was particularly amused by the old world habit of kissing of ladies' hands with a great flourish or clicking of heels at greetings. It was especially odd, to see this kind of mannerisms in the proverbially reserved country, like England, it offered such contrast. The club with its restaurant remained opened for some years to come and I used to visit and eat there with my brothers and their friends, on my visits to England, until Ludwik declared that the food there was no longer addible. I will always miss the place with its highly charged atmosphere and the misplaced old world charm. A large number of the members of the Polish army in Great

Britain who did not return home, settled there as the names in the London telephone book can attest. Now the second and third generation is well integrated into the British way of life.

To be in London at the age of nineteen, with out any basic financial restrictions, due to generosity of my brothers, was joy and a privilege. In retrospect, how right was Wordsworth in saying "If a man is tired of London, he is tired of life". And I certainly was not tired of London! On my frequent visits there or on an extended leave, I would eagerly seek or be exposed to many different events and people, many of which have left a lasting impact on me. Just living in our flat led to meeting some varied and occasionally very interesting people. Most were friends or soldier acquaintances of my brothers spending their furlough in London. Some would come from as far as Germany or France. There would be sometimes as many as, a dozen guests at one time, often spending the night there, sleeping all over the place, including the floors. Food was still rationed in the early post war months, so they would bring such food with them as eggs, butter, sausage and the like. I would cook rather sumptuous breakfasts and very much enjoyed the general camaraderie, although most of the men were older than I.

One result of Ludwiks' readily offered hospitality was the presence in our flat for some time of the family Singer. Bernard Singer was a much-respected editor of a national newspaper, in Poland. He and his family survived the war in France from where they arrived to settle in England. Having nowhere to stay and being financially strapped, they were given refuge in our flat, for the time being. This lead to a most exciting political awakening and education that left a lasting impression on me. I had the unusual opportunity to listen to extensive political discussions which often took place between Bernard Singer and his friends. The two whom I remember best were, Isaac Deutcher who at that time was a political correspondent for" The Observer," a respected English newspaper. He subsequently wrote the definitive biographies of Stalin and Trotzki. The other was Bernard Helft. There were others, but I cannot clearly recall them. The important fact however, was that they were radical socialists, adherents of Trotzki. They were extremely well acquainted with the Bolshevik political credo, the Kommitern and the life of the Kremlin inner circle. At that time London was in a political turmoil, as some the seminal discussions relating to formation and organization of

the United Nations, took place there. The two opposing power blocks were the Soviet Union and the West, lead by America. Leading the Russian delegation was the infamous prosecutor of the Moscow trials in the thirties, Andrzej Wyszinski (Vishinski). Singer and his group would analyze daily these discussions. What amazed me most was their uncanny accuracy with which they predicted Vishinsky's responses and proposals. I sat at their feet with eager attention, when ever I could, sensing what a special intellectual and political opportunity it was for me, to be so enlightened.

Many years later Bernard Helft was very kind to Edith and me, when on our arrival to Canada, he let us stayed in their small apartment, crowded with their newly born child. I do not think that his wife ever forgave him. It was also in Montreal, that I have met later, Isaac Deutcher once again, when he was there on his book tour. By that time he was also a renowned political author. Not so long ago, I had the opportunity to speak with Bernard singer's son who was the Paris correspondent for the Nation magazine. He was here to chair a meeting of a Socialist organization, which name escapes me. We renewed our acquaintance after some fifty years hiatus.

My first theatre experience happen inadvertently, on one sunny Sunday afternoon when walking in the Regents Park, I stumbled on the open air performance of "A Midsummer's' Night Dream". It was also my first awareness of Shakespeare. It certainly was some awaking for me, no pun intended. The next time my brush with his writing was by reading the "Lamb's Tales of Shakespeare", but my serious interest and pleasure, began with "As You Like It". It was this play, which we studied in depth, in the matriculation course I took in South Africa. From that time on, I took every opportunity to see his plays, including several performances at Stafford on Avon, which were indeed, very special theatrical experiences.

Before I describe my life in London, I must admit of being acutely aware of the good fortune that brought us, the three Kleiner brothers back together and to a feeling of great elation whenever the three of us would walk in unison the streets of this wonderful and welcoming city.

After some months spent in Kinghorn, I was relocated to a small town farther north, famous for its whisky mills. It was there that I felt particularly lonely, although it was a pleasant town on a river. Paradoxically instead being housed in the wooden barracks, this time we occupied a very pleasant chateau surrounded by nice grounds. This was only a temporary station, until we were transferred to the west coast, to Inveraray. It was a rather long train ride, during which I was assured by a Scott, who shared my compartment, that all I can expect for company there, were sheep. He was not half wrong. Inveraray, was a tiny hamlet at the end of an inlet referred to as Loch in Scottish. It was so small that it even lacked the ubiquitous Fish and Chip shop, but oddly enough, it had a small hotel with a restaurant. It was however the seat of the Duke of Inveraray, with the customary, imposing, but dreary castle to prove it. The base to my surprise was quite extensive.

Once more, I was unexpectedly privileged, by the presence there of the father of Ludwik's best friend. Dr. Lifszyc was a dentist on the base, with the rank of Captain. It was his son of his who gave Ludwik the money for the ticket for the trans Siberian train journey, while my rich uncle Herman refused to help. The irony was that while this act of kindness helped my brother escape Soviet Russia, the younger Lifszyc died three hours after the German surrender, which ended the war in Europe. He as a navigator and his pilot were lost without a trace flying a Mosquito form Belgium to their base in England. Dr. Lifszyc arranged for me to serve as his orderly, the benefit of it was that I was housed in the officers' quarters and had a lot of privacy. One of the more comical experiences I had there, was when one evening I was sent by Dr, Lifszyc to get some cigarettes at the officers' canteen. It was quite foggy and cold so I throw a heavy army coat over my shoulders, which incidentally covered my rank designation, which was that of a lowly Private. As I was standing at the bar waiting to buy the cigarettes, I was approached by a slightly inebriated Lieutenant, demanding my rank by asking if I too was an officer, as the canteen was off limits to the likes of me. Therefore, when he addressed me in a form of a question as if I too were of the same rank, I answered no, Captain, at which time he saluted smartly and turned on his heal. I did so in all innocence as I assumed he was asking me, who sent me there.

Other things which amused me no end, and believe me one needed some diversions when you lived there, was my function as the Cyrano de Bergerac, to some of the soldiers, who could neither read nor write English. I would write their letters in English to the girlfriends and then had to read and translate their replies. We also played many sports, as there was literarily nothing else to do. There was none of the usual need for training, as we were no longer expected to fight, so we merely vegetated until such time, when the anticipated demobilization will come. One Sunday when I set in a gazebo at the inlet of the Loch, a woman whom I felt to be quite old, by my standards, set next to me. In the course in the conversation, I understood that she is visitor to Inverrary where she came to see her boyfriend on our base. When upon hearing that, I raised my eyebrows in surprise, as I knew that most of the soldiers were young, to which she responded in a slightly haughty manner: "Young man, the older the fiddle, the better the tune". It was one more lessons of life, to be neither too presumptuous nor judgmental. I left the gazebo with the tail between my legs.

Despite the long distances, I continued to visit London, but this time the train left from Glasgow. First however, was a long ride form the base to the city which we usually accomplished, for some reason in an ambulance. On the way, whenever we passed Loch Lommond, we would honor it, by bursting out singing the well-known ballad of this lake. We were not always in unison or on pitch, but we certainly sang with great spirit and vigor. Finally, the day arrived when after being honorably demobilized in Greenock, near Glasgow, I left for London.

My Brothers even before they knew of my survival had applied to immigrate to South Africa. Although Ludwik had some contacts in the States, with promise of sponsorship, they decided not to go to America. I think that this was, even in retrospect a brilliant decision. To start life in the States, with only modest resources, would have been in all likelihood been far more difficult for us. The Passage to South Africa was almost impossible to obtain. So much so, than Bob in a very cavalier fashion seriously considered buying a Pier Cub, a two-seater plane to travel there. It ended up, however, with Bob because of his heroic war service, obtained a sea passage on a steamer for him and me. Ludwik was to remain in England until such time until we get our bearings in Johannesburg.

Land of the Lotus Eaters

From Liverpool to Cape Town

We left England from Liverpool on the western coast. I was quite overwhelmed by the prospect that soon I shall be in some far off land, leaving Europe forever. Having a choice of remaining in Great Britain, for me however, was not an option. I became dubious about the viability of peace and personal freedoms, fearing that the escalating political confrontations between the West and Soviet dominated East may flare up into another European conflict. Such distant countries as the USA or South Africa I thought, might offer a more stable environment, having naively assumed that distance equated with security. There was a point of view I often heard voiced, that when "America gets a cold, Europe gets Pneumonia" yet I was very I happy and excited by the prospects of seeing new Worlds. South Africa in particular was a welcome prospect, as I having recently heard of the great quality of life there. I also recalled that as child I was given a richly illustrated book about the Boer War and its hero Paul Kruger. A particular incidence, in which Paul Kruger amputating his own thumb, so impressed me at the time, it stuck with me forever. I looked on this opportunity for a new life there, as a great adventure and was immensely grateful to my brothers for making it possible.

Our boat was a relatively small freighter of only twelve thousand tons, which name escapes me, but I remember that it sailed under the flag of the Blue Star Lines. I must admit that I was a little anxious of how I would withstand a three-week long journey on board ship without standard amenities. I was especially fearful of the seasickness. I was warned in particular about the Irish Sea and the rollers of the Bay of Biscayne. Well, only the Irish Sea proved true to its reputation and more. The rest of the passage was filled with sunny days, starry nights and flying fish cavorting across the bow. We were given rather simple quarters on the stern of the boat and we ate with the crew. We stopped on the way at Tenerife on the Canary Islands off the coast of Africa. It was an exotic location with Palm trees; Africa as I had imagined. My brother Bob wore his Air Force uniform, so that throughout the day we were followed by the Spanish Militia. Keep in mind that at that time, the Dictator Franco

governed Spain and its possessions. Throughout the war he was on the side of the Axis Countries, but was not formally engaged in combat against the Allies, except for a small contingent of soldiers on the Eastern front, in Russia. We were more amused than threatened by this surveillance. I was impressed by the relative abundance of food and goods, as compared to the post war Britain. There were a great variety of leather goods available. Bob bought a really elegant suitcase in cream-colored leather with a smaller case for accessories, as a present for Audrey, his future wife.

The rest of the voyage was smooth and uneventful. I must say that I was never bored despite the fact that there was nothing much to do on board. I think we did physical exercise, played cards and read some. We arrived into Cape Town harbor on a clear October day, without a cloud in the sky, except for the famous milky cloth over Table Mountain. This traditional sight was a most welcoming omen. Even the waters of the bay, which can be frequently very rough and known as the Cape Rollers, were smooth that day. Visually Cape Town and its environs are considered one of the great sights of the world. Indeed, it so appeared to us that day. Wisely, Bob decided to spend a few days in the city before we were to leave for Johannesburg. We settled at a modest hotel in town. Had the budget allowed, the famous Mount Nelson in all its pink glory at the end of a long driveway with the row of very impressive royal palms on either side, would have been our choice. I did make a vow to come back in the future and stay there. It took many years but on one of our trips to South Africa, Edith and I, did indeed have an occasion to enjoy this famous hotel for a few days. What made an instantaneous impression on me was the obvious material wellbeing of the country, as compared to Europe after the war. It was the presence of the massive American cars in large numbers and the seven course meals offered in most restaurants. One of the lasting memories was eating the enormous ice cream sundaes topped with fresh fruit. What was particularly fascinating for me was that for the first time in my life I was in the midst of people of many colors and strange tongues. The weather was simply lovely that October. Just strolling on the streets of this beautiful city, was a great pleasure. Once again in choosing our means of getting to Johannesburg, Bob made a wise decision to travel in style. One never knew if such an opportunity would ever again arise for us, so we boarded the famously luxurious Blue Train. The twenty-four hour journey to Jo-burg (common abbreviation for

Johannesburg) was memorable. The train passed through the beautiful countryside of the Cape, which included the spectacular wine country. I still remember the service and food as well as the compartment's furnishings. It was then in one of the elegant club cars that I tasted Sherry for the first time and have enjoyed it ever since.

Johannesburg – The Early Days

As we were approaching the outskirts of Jo-burg, I noticed when looking out of the train windows, many mine damps along the way. They resembled rectangular pyramids with a flat top, like an inverted cake pan. They were uniformly yellow, and in a way, they were them selves emblematic of the character of this city. Jo-burg not only was the City of Gold as it was generally called, but in fact, it was a golden city. To my regret, many years later I had the occasion to visit again and the mine damps were either diminished in size or overgrown with weeds or disappeared altogether. There was however, a downside to their presence in the early day. They were very close to the city proper, so when the wind blew, every thing was covered by a very fine sand, which in all probability must have contain, some toxic chemical and traces of heavy metals.

Within a very short time of our arrival, Bob very energetically found a place to live. The studio apartment was in a small building of flats at one end of Commissioner Street, which was on the main commercial drag of the city. In the same building, was a small café where we often ate. It was run by a couple, Josef and Marisia Rosenberg, recent immigrants from Poland. We became good friends. My first memory of the apartment was, when looking through an open window, I noticed a group of small "pickenins" (native African children), dancing rhythmically in unison to the beat of their song. This was my first experience of the very special inborn characteristic talents of the Native African. Now with Miriam Makeba, as well as several well-known African singing and dancing groups, especially the archipelago choirs, they have become renown and enjoyed through out the world.

The very next thing that we did was to inquire about the educational possibilities for me. By then I was nineteen, with a seven-year hiatus from formal schooling, speaking only passable

colloquial English. The Damian College, a rather prestigious name for a private cram school, was suggested as a potential solution. It was primarily for those students who failed at formal schools, had behavioral problems or needed additional tutoring to pass the all-important Matriculation examination, essential for a university admission. Bob went with me for an interview with the director of the college to inquire if I would be allowed to join the matriculating class in the following February. By then it was already the end of October. The director, after reviewing my history, was dubious if this was at all doable. He did suggest that I should have a special tutor if I really wanted to give it try. He recommended that I should undergo a period of intense study of only a few subjects. If at the end of that time, I decided to submit to another assessment interview, he may consider admitting me to the college. He also stressed that the opinion of the tutor would be all-important in arriving at a sensible decision. The tutor, Mr. Kriel, proved to be a gem of a teacher. He mainly concentrated on English and its literature, math, physics and chemistry. I was so grateful for this opportunity to be in school again, that in spite of the rather heavy schedule, I inhaled it all and loved it. I surprised myself, as previously I was really a very mediocre student. My strongest motivation, which speared me on, was the possible chance of an opportunity for a University education.

In February of 1947, I was admitted into Damien College. Most of the students were slightly younger than I, but it felt good being among them and having them as my friends. One special boy, who befriended me, was Jonathan Friedman. He was the son of a member of the South African parliament, a man who was regarded with respect and was considered one of its most articulate speakers. Johnathan's mother was a published poet of some recognition. He had a sister Gillian, then still a schoolgirl at Rodean Academy. I had a serious crush on her while I was in Medical School. Jonathan was a rather small slender person, with a snooty air of intellectual superiority. He did not thrive at the prestigious school he previously attended. My feeling was that in large measure he probably had an inferiority complex, which might have been caused by failing to meet parental expectations. For me, however, by associating with him, I was offered a great opportunity to be exposed to a higher cultural and intellectual milieu. The few times that I was invited to dinner, I would sit in awe listening to the conversation around the table between the Friedmans' and their guests. Jonathan was well

read and had a deep appreciation and knowledge of serious music. He made disparaging remarks when I voiced my admiration for Chopin, while he would praise such modern composers as Hindemith. His parents were wealthy and lived in a mansion in Lower Houghton, then the prime suburb of Jo-burg. I must admit being grateful for having him for a friend, though he was not an easy person to be around. He was cynical and somewhat bitter, but he enlarged my horizons with limitations that were rather obvious. For many years I did not know what had become of him, as he left for England soon after the untimely death of both his parents. Only recently, I was made aware that he might have committed suicide. Gillian, after finishing school, hung out with a group of people who could be best described as hippies. These were young people with intellectual pretensions who were believed to be heavy into drugs, which in South Africa was mainly Dagha (local version of Marijuana). They probably used other drugs as well. She also ended up in England where she married Bekker, the ringleader of the group. She apparently became a published author, writing a bitterly critical book about her parents.

In the meantime, Bob was at loose ends until the arrival of Audrey. Up to then we were meeting people and making friends, most of whom like us, were from Poland. One such family who had a big, open house, and who were most hospitable were the Gonskies. My daily life presented sharp contrasts to that of my recent experiences in Europe, especially because of the Master-Servant way of life in South Africa. At first, I remember being slightly embarrassed, when on the very day we arrived in Jo-burg we were invited to the Reins, a family of Ludwik's best friend from the army. I asked if I may go to the kitchen for a glass of water, which I was firmly denied. I was told to wait so that their servant could bring me one. On another occasion we were invited for an evening pool party at the house of a Mr. "Marble Bottom Levin". Intrigued by an unusual moniker, we eagerly went. We found ourselves at party of people by a beautiful blue-green marble swimming pool, lit effectively from the inside. The reason for the nickname then became obvious. Many people in our social sphere had homes on at least one acre, with fine gardens, swimming pools and tennis courts and of course Black servants. The ideal climate, also contributed to the general sense of well being. Indeed, I thought that it was then the Land of the Lotus Eaters. But things were soon to change.

The first year in Jo-burg, besides my being totally engrossed in my schooling and making friends and acquaintances, was marked by several other events. The most important was the marriage of Bob and Audrey at the Johannesburg City Hall, which almost did not happen. On that very day, the British Royal Family with the two young Princesses in tow, were visiting the city. It was at a time when security was nearly non-existent. They could walk along the streets of Johannesburg with the sidewalks lined by enthusiastically cheering crowds. Other assorted Government officials marched behind them, followed by a parade. This meant that we could not get to the court unless one took a major detour, which we did, having arrived breathless and panting on the steps of city hall only moments before it was suppose to close. Using a car on that day was not an option. We traipsed to the Zoo Lake restaurant for a celebratory dinner of a pork chop dish named for its fancy sauce, "Bernard". The South African cuisine was not known at that time for its excellence. Within a short time, Bob bought a modest house in the Northern part of Jo-burg, in a new development in Parkhurst. Ludwik, who arrived to South Africa a month or so later, lived with me in a flat near my Medical School. I do not recall Bob working consistently at that time, but Ludwik very quickly found a job in a wholesale clothing business as a traveling salesmen, a type of work of which he had no previous experience. Working for Mr. Marks was not a bed of roses, to say the least. It was a classic case of exploitation of a "Greener", as newly arrived immigrants were called in the world of cut and trim, on Market Street in Johannesburg. The job consisted of traveling extensively within a wide radius, often as much as several hundred miles over country roads. He was given a driver, an old car, suitcases full of samples and a list of customers. Ludwik proved to be a quick study and was well liked by the people he met. He left Mr. Marks' establishment and opened his own firm "Kleiner Bros." with the trade .mark "Brewster Products". Bob now had meaningful employment as the inside man of the firm. Ludwik continued for some time both as the salesman, as well as a buyer and the financial manager. It was a tall order, but he thrived on it and very soon he developed this in to a substantial business with a number of employees. On occasions, I too liked to help. One of the pivotal workers was an African of mixed racial background. He was a mix of Hottentot and Bushmen. Both these ancient, disparate ethnic groups bore a strong resemblance to the early Homo Sapiens inhabiting the Southern tip of Africa. Most anthropologists considered

them to be the original inhabitants, before the massive migration of the Bantu from the North displaced them. He was a small man with a well rounded head, so typical of the Bushmen. He was an energetic, smart, loyal and just a very likable guy. We felt no racial or social differences between us. He was indispensable to the firm and stayed with us until we left the country.

The other burden Ludwik took upon himself was to provide total financial support for the three of us. My contribution was literally nil, until I could fend for a myself, which had to wait until I graduated from Medical School. Up to that time. I was given this extraordinary financial and moral support to pursue my studies in total freedom from want, for which I remained grateful to my brothers forever.

Ludwik on his arrival to South Africa and for some time after was not at all certain that he liked it here and considered going back to England. Both Bob and I were totally enthusiastic about our new lifestyle. Ludwig did, however, made many friends quickly, especially among the Polish crowd, with poker and bridge as standard entertainment. Bob and Audrey were much more reserved, leaning toward the English groups. One of Bob's friends from the Air Force Days was an elegant and charming Englishman, a nephew of Edith Sitwell, a respected author and an intellectual of the day. I managed to float between these two worlds, which often were worlds apart. One of the residues of the British colonialism was the unbearable snootiness and social pretensions, particularly of those recent middle class English immigrants. The South Africans in contrast were very democratic and socially undiscriminating as long as you were White and interesting.

As I was nearing the end of my schooling, a decision had to be made of what I should do next. I must admit of being quite unfocussed as to my next goal, so when one of our friends suggested Medicine, I eagerly embraced the idea without having any previous interest in such discipline. This was not one of those lifelong romanticized career decisions, altruistically motivated, but rather a simple choice. Not only did I learn to love medicine but it truly became my life calling and fulfillment, not unlike an arranged marriage, which in the end leads to mutual affection.

Getting to a Medical School, proved however to be a major challenge. Having passed my matriculation exam, my first choice was the English speaking Wiwatersrand University in Johannesburg. As an ex-service man, I was supposed to get priority consideration for admission, where only ten percent of candidates were chosen out of twelve hundred. I eagerly went for my interview with the registrar of the Medical School, only to be rejected out of hand by the man, a Mr. Pollock. To my astonishment, he stated that because I was a veteran of the Polish army, I did not deserve any special consideration. When I retorted that the Poles were under British command, he started raving against them based on an experience he had with them when he was in the army in Italy. Dejected, not knowing whom to turn to for help, I applied to an Afrikaans speaking University in Pretoria, which had an open admission policy.

"***We Are Marching to Pretoria…***"

There were three capital cities in South Africa, each with a specific functional designation. Pretoria was one of these capitals. It was the seat of the Administrative Government for half the year, while the other six months was spent in Cape Town, a thousand miles away, where the Parliament convened. The Judiciary Capital was in Bloemfontein, in the heart of the country. Pretoria was predominantly populated by the Boers otherwise known as Afrikaners, who were the early pioneers. They were the descendants of the Dutch with a mixture of the French Huguenots and some German stock. What they did not admit to, was the rather strong evidence of the traces of the African and Malay genes, because racial mixing was strictly taboo from the very inception of the country. Pretoria was known for the imposing Government buildings by a renowned British colonial architect. Its streets were lined with the Jacaranda trees, which was quite a sight when they bloomed in the spring. Otherwise, it was a rather less than exciting city. It was hot in the summer and cold in the winter. One of those unfathomable facts about the South Africans was that they failed to recognize how very cold it could get in the unheated homes on the High Veld of Transvaal, in mid-winter. What was especially irksome was that many rooms had airbricks letting in cold drafts. I rented a cell of a room on the patio of a house with a rather simple Afrikaner family and arranged to

eat my meals at a nearby boarding house, where the company was good but the food was awful. The life at the Pretoria University Medical School was very difficult for a number of reasons. At the time when my English finally became acceptable, I had to learn some basic Afrikaans to follow the lectures and to be able to write exams. There were no medical books in that language. After reading the prescribed books in English, I then had to translate the contents into Afrikaans, so as to be able to participate meaningfully in class or to be able to write exams. Afrikaans was not yet a literary language, but a patois based on Dutch with some admixture of German and with a few anglicized words. It was a surprisingly easy to learn, as it had a simple grammar and a rather reinforcing charming double negative. On some occasions when flustered, I would speak in all four languages at once. What Afrikaans I learned was in large measure due to my landlady who spoke no English. She was quite pleasant and occasionally invited me to join them for the occasional Sunday meal. It was very obvious that she and her family were strong Nazi sympathizers during the war, as was the bulk of the Afrikaners. As it was only 1948, memories of the war were still very fresh in their minds with the unwelcome victory by the British and their allies. Although generally she was quite congenial, she could be quite cruel to her black maid. One such incident which upset me no end was, when I witnessed her dunking forcefully the young women's head into a toilet bowl, because she did something the old women did not like.

The lectures and the subsequent examinations were brutal. Because of the policy of open admissions, they discriminated only at the end, when out of the class of three hundred, only thirty students passed, some of whom were repeaters of the year before. I passed Botany, Physics and Biology but failed Chemistry, as did most of the class. The professor was the designated "Madam de Farges" of the school. The course in Chemistry was purposely designed to fail the great majority of the class. It was divided in three separate sections, consisting of Organic, Inorganic and Physical Chemistry. The level of difficulty can be best described by the type of questions asked, where for example we were expected to give six different methods of salt preparations. We had to write three hourly written examinations, one for each of the different sections. Holtz was a professor of the old school. He was thoroughly German in his national background and in his pedantic attitude. I believe that he was interned during the war as a probable Nazi, which might have farther embittered him.

Needless to say this arrogant, small gnome of a man was feared by all the students. I was at a loss as to what should I do in the coming year. Do I go back to Pretoria and risk another failure? I bitterly remembered the rejection from Wits (Witwatersrand University) which I thought unfair and decided to seek a redress. It was fortuitous that one of Ludwik's friends knew the Vice Chancellor of the university and arranged a personal interview for me. Professor Glen Thomas was well known for his liberal views. On hearing about my encounter with the Registrar the year before and on confirming my version of the incidence, Dr..Pollock was removed from his post. To my great joy, I was admitted to the Wits Medical School for the coming academic year. One happy family event, which happened during the time I spent in Pretoria, was the birth of my nephew Robert. It was particularly meaningful for me, as it was an affirmation of survival, now that a new generation of Kleiners' was born.

The Salad Days

The year of 1948 was a most extraordinary time in my life in terms of growth, development and sheer joy. Not only was I admitted to Wits, which meant so much to me, but I was given exemptions for all the three subjects which I had already previously passed. I was only required to repeat chemistry, which after the stringent requirements at Pretoria University, was a breeze at Wits. In fact, it was the only first class pass, equivalent to honors, which I ever received throughout my academic career. With much time on my hands, I became involved in student extra-curricular activities on campus. As I was older than most of my classmates, I naturally gravitated toward the more mature elder students, particularly those doing a B.A. and not the Sciences. I was free to attend many cultural activities sponsored by the University such as special lectures, musical events and plays, both as an audience, as well the occasional participant. One such event was a medieval English play, the name escapes me, in which Edith played the title role of a queen, and I was only the lowly spear-carrier. The irony of it was that we discovered being in the same play, only much later.

I was also fortunate to have among some of my friends, knowledgeable and talented students. They often took it upon themselves to expose me to music and included me when they attended concerts and musicals. At one such event, the program consisted of a new work of

composition by a student. I commented to the amusement of my more sophisticated companions, that to me it sounded like "accidental" music. They thought I was making a witty criticism of the piece. What I really meant to say, which I latter admitted, was that it sounded like "incidental music" where upon they started laughing in earnest at my faux pas. As it turned out, one of those friends that night was Ivan Melman, even then already a promising pianist, who later won the coveted Grand Prize in the Queen Elisabeth of Belgium competition. Despite the unbridgeable divide in our appreciation and knowledge of music, he was not only tolerant of my musical naiveté, but was quite happy to accompany me one evening on the piano, while I attempted a vocal rendition in German of Goethe's Earl Koenig. Also that year I got involved with a group students who were making a silent film, based on the novella by James Joyce: "The Portrait of the Author as young Man". Besides it being great fun, it turned out to be an interesting experience and made me appreciate some of the challenges in filmmaking. I was given the part of the barman, a somewhat villainous role. It was shown that year at a local film competition, winning the first prize, out of three presented. I also had an opportunity to sit in on lectures on the History and Philosophy of Science, which I found of great interest.

Outside the campus, there was a multitude of other activities. Tennis was played year round, while swimming was fun only in the summer, unless there was a heated pool. The level of hospitality was extraordinarily generous, either in peoples' homes or in their gardens. The pool parties were especially popular. The cinema was an important part of entertainment and frequented often. It was quite a big deal, in the sense, that it consisted of number of features and the tickets had to be booked ahead of time. Every show started by standing up and singing "God Save the King" substituted later by Queen, of course. A box of chocolate was mandatory if a girl was coming along, which often was frequently the case. Dancing and nightclubs were very popular, even among the students. Keep in mind that this was a very well to do community and exclusively European, as the Whites were known then, while the Blacks were referred to as Natives. Kaffer was the worse form of derogatory name calling of the Native South African, although its derivation was from an Arabic word for a Non-believer. Roi Nek or Red Neck was the offensive word to designate any British, not so much for their social behavior, as much for the propensity of their white skin to get sunburned.

The live theatre was very exciting and ambitious, with lots of serious local talent and an occasional imported, but fading star from England. These visiting actors had to go by boat which was the only available means of traveling from Europe in those days and it took a minimum of two weeks. Neither the less, we saw the likes of Danny Kay or heard Johnny Ray the crying singer and his band. Serious musicians of the caliber of Yehudi Menuchin or famous Italian opera singers would appear from time to time. On rare occasions, a major British orchestra under the baton of such conductors of note, as Sir Thomas Beecham, would conduct a national tour of South Africa. One surprising cultural tradition was the serious national interest in Ballet, which was taught in most towns, regardless of size or sophistication. Apparently, one or two great teachers by the former members of the Ballet Rouse, started this trend. Kranko, one of the most famous chorographers of the post war period, was a young man from Johannesburg. He also just happened to be a nephew of a Mr. Kranko, who had typewriters repair shop I would occasionally visit on business, for my brothers. Edith and I saw him backstage one evening in New York, after attending his Company's performance and we reminisced about the early days in Johannesburg. Sadly he died three days later of an unknown cause, while flying back to Europe. It was considered a tragic loss for the World of Ballet at large.

One of the great events of X-mass season was the annual Pantomime, A silly affair imported from England each year but eagerly appreciated by the locals, as it was in the Mother Country. Cross-dressing and bathroom jokes were the main stays of such a performance. Even in those days we did not subscribe to it.

I happen to be writing this segment during the holidays' season, which reminds me of my first X-mass in South Africa. I was invited to spend my vacation at some friend's home in Bloemfontein. The town which name translates as the Fountain of Flowers was a few hundred miles southeast from Johannesburg in the low Veld, a very hot part of the country in summer. The town was the surrounded by farm communities, therefore it was predominantly Afrikaans. Its claim to fame was, as I have mentioned before, that after the creation of the Union of South Africa, Bloemfontein became its Judicial Capital. Although there was very

little of interest for a young man like myself, the boredom was eased by company of two different women, one younger the other slightly older than I. The first was a very talented Ballet dancer; the other was a very well read and an interesting person.

The people I stayed with were most hospitable and generous. The three meals a day defy description, because of the infinite variety and copious amount of food. I am sad to say that most members of the family died at a relatively early age, from heart disease which in retrospect was not surprising. The X-mass day was spent on a checkbook farm, of a rich manufacturer from Durban. As it was the beginning of summer, the party was outside centered on the traditional Brei Fleis, otherwise known as the barbecue. The heavy eating and drinking, followed by a massive exodus for a swim in the nearby dam, ended for me with an equally massive discomfort, on entering the water. The admonition not to swim immediately after a meal was never more apt, than at that time.

A year later I was invited to spend a few days on the same farm, at which time I was very lucky to have escaped a serious accident. They had a stable of horses and being a game for any adventure, I accepted the invitation to go riding with their English governess. She was there to look after my host's, two young daughters. She was a handsome woman and obviously a good rider. I was given a former racehorse to ride with a saddle little too small for comfort, and a warning that on the way back to the stables, the horse may be difficult to control. The ride into the country was pleasant enough. After a small picnic, I tried to remount for the way back, but as soon as I placed my left foot into the stirrup, the horse was off at a gallop, with me hanging on frantically to the horse's mane, for dear life. I also I lost the bridle and as hard as tried, I could not get my foot into the right stirrup .I arrived at the stable in record time, barely managed to avoid becoming the headless horseman. I escaped a serious head injury, by bending down low, only a few short seconds before the horse flew under the low gate. I am still baffled how I was lucky to avoid falling off the horse on the way there and escaped being decapitated. I did not come of it unscathed however, having received multiple cuts, bruises on the inner thighs, and have lost whatever I had in my pockets along the pathway. I must admit that this was neither my first nor the last horse miss-adventure. When I was still in London, I heard of the famous bridle path, the Rotten Row in

the Hyde Park. At that time, I still had my ridding boots and jodhpurs, but having never been on a horse before, I was keen to try it. A few days previously, I saw people ridding beautiful horses, dressed for the occasion and a silver handled crop in their hands. It was a scene reminiscent of the ubiquitous reproductions of English life commonly seen on the walls of clubs or pretentious private libraries. Having located a stable, I had no trouble renting a horse, but I trying to get on to the saddle, of this tall animal, was more of a challenge than I anticipated. By the time, I having finally succeeded, after numerous attempts, the group with which I was supposed to ride with, was by then, well ahead of me. It was a blessing in disguise, as I at least have avoided the embarrassment, of having the temerity even to try, being totally devoid of any previous experience riding a horse. The third and last of my horse misadventures took place in a Boys Scouts camp in the Laurentians, north of Montreal. I was the camp doctor there the previous summer and Edith, our infant Child and I were invited for a long weekend. A very fine horse with an English saddle, was stabled nearby our cottage, so once more, I was led into a temptation. I was told that the proper way to ride a horse with such a saddle is to rise with the rhythms of the horse's steps, which meant slight lifting using ones thighs. This time I almost learned some fundamentals of horse back ridding and was rather pleased with myself. The back pay came the night as I have developed painful spasms of my inner thighs, from the repetitive lifting in the stirrups. The only comfort of sorts was provided by my baby's milk bottle, filled with hot water

At the end of the academic year, which in South Africa falls in December, I went to Durban for the winter vacation. It was a popular sea site resort, besides being an important commercial port, on the Indian Ocean. It was a favorite spot for holidays, when the rest of the country was wet or cold. It was known for its fine beaches, warm climate in the wintertime and the danger of sharks. It was there, when a visiting French girl caused a sensation by wearing a bikini while, we were walking on the beach. I was not sure whether to be embarrassed or pleased by all this attention, as such a skimpy bathing suit was seen there only for the very first time.

Being now able to live in Johannesburg again, having spent such rewarding and enjoyable year at the Witwatersrand University having acquired interesting friends and a myriad of new

experiences, was for me nothing short of an illusion, of living the life, of the Student Prince from a Romberg's Operetta.

On my return to Johannesburg from the summer vacations, the studying started in earnest. The second year at the Medical School consisted of courses in Anatomy and Physiology. The school was outside the main university campus, some distant away, adjacent to the Johannesburg General Hospital, which then consisted of separate Black and White facilities. Also by that time the Nationalist Party, was firmly entrenched, having unexpectedly won the National Parliamentary elections. It's members were almost entirely Afrikaners (Boers) with an agenda to separate the various colored racial groups from the Whites and from one another. Thus, the word Apartheid found its way in to the international lexicon. Although there was clearly social, economic and political discrimination throughout the country prior to the Nationalist Government coming into power, there was now however, an institutionally mandated systematic isolation of the Blacks, the Coloreds (mix race of Malays, Blacks and Whites) and the Indians. What ever even the small social or political privileges, which they might have enjoyed before this national election, were now significantly restricted. The Blacks were removed to territories according to their tribal origins. The Indians and the Colords were had to move to designated areas of habitation, which fact these were Ghettos without walls. Social interaction was frowned upon. Marriages or mixing of sexes between whites and the others was against the law, punishable by prison. Those Black Africans who remained as part of the vital work force, did so on special Passes, while their families had to return to their designated Home Lands. The great hardships resulted from the forced separation and repatriation was unconscionable. Yet having this large mass of relatively poor workers benefited equally those Whites, who were both for and against apartheid. The political opposition was in the hands of the United Party, then consisting of English speaking groups predominantly those from Great Britain, some who have been in South Africa for generations. There was a prominent segment of the more educated, affluent Afrikaners like General Smuts, who at one time was the President of the country and Jan Hofmayer, the Prime Minister. They were the leaders when the United Party was in power, while many others who were senior members of the government or the civil service. It was under the leadership of Jan Smuts however, that the elections were lost by the United Party, in large

measure because of his overconfidence. The high hopes and the optimism for a great future and the possible gradual resolution of the serious racial shortcomings of the country, when I arrived to South Africa, were suddenly extinguished. A government of dour, black hated, somber leaders of the Dutch Reformed Church, sons of the Voortrekers, the early pioneers, took over the government excluding all others. The dislike of the British which for many Afrikaners bordered on hate, was in large measure due to the residue of their defeat in the Boer War, when the civilian population was apparently severely mistreated. It was also then that the British pioneered the concept of Concentration Camps. Other residue of the Boer War which entered the international lexicon were the words such as "Commandos" and "Khaki" With the political victory the Afrikaners rekindled their bitter memories of those days. With subsequent gerrymandering of the voting districts, they made it impossible for the United Party, to ever again win another election. The history of Apartheid is well known, but I just wanted to give my own short version of it.

The University of Witwatersrand and its Medical School had a policy of admitting students regardless of color, religion or race, although I am suspicious that to some degree, there were restrictions for Blacks, minorities and women, as we had precisely ten percent of each in most classes. Unlike the society outside, the University however, fostered a very free social interaction between all groups of students, as long as it was limited to the campus. It meant that we ate together in the cafeteria, played cards, shared benches in the lecture halls, but never socialized outside the university. The Black students were not allowed the use of the university swimming pool nor attend Post Mortem on White Patients. The "Diener" as the attendant in the morgue handling the bodies was known as, was of course black. A similar paradox existed at the railroad at stations, where the entrances were clearly marked as for Blacks or whites only, but they could not avoid mixing on reaching the platform. These are only some examples of the insanities of this system. It was a bitter irony that these policies were put in force, so soon after the defeat of the Nazi Germany and their racial laws. How could the civilized world tolerate this system for so many years!

I have made a bunch of new friends on the campus of the Medical School but the most outstanding individual, was Albert Kuschlick. He was the youngest and probably one of the

smartest students in the class. He was somewhat swarthy, with a pockmarked face yet bordering handsome, with a somewhat lazy pattern of speech, but was quite charming.. His father, a Professor of Physics at Wits influenced Albert by his leftist leaning views to a degree, that Albert eventually became identified by the police, as a Communist, a member of a political party not allowed by the Nationalist Government. This did not come to pass however, until he graduated from the Medical School and left the country just short of being arrested. As the years progressed, we became life long friends. We have studied together each year for the final annual examinations, which was most fortunate for me. I felt that it helped me pass and I give him credit for it. He had a blind believe in the Communist Manifesto and looked to the Soviet Union as the Bastion of Freedom. How such a smart man could sustain an unshakable believe even after Stalin' death and the denunciation by Krushchev, was difficult for me to accept. The friendship did not suffer because of our political differences. After leaving South Africa, he became very active in the international youth organizations sponsored by the Russians. Eventually he settled permanently in England, where after farther medical studies he became a worldwide, recognized expert on Autism. We did have occasions to meet each other through the years, either on his visits to America or when we were in England. He had a difficult and somewhat unhappy personal life, having lost his first wife in an airplane accident. She was a very bright women, who was a Labor Party member in the British Parliament. Albert, like his father died a premature death from heart disease.

It was through Albert, that I met Edith. We were invited to the house of our Professor of Pharmacology, for dinner, although I usually had a number of girlfriends, I could not get a date for that evening. Albert at that time was going steady with a girl by the name Pamela, who shared digs with Edith. With a wounded ego, I accepted this blind date. To my great surprise and great pleasure, I met a most charming, articulate, attractive eighteen-year old girl, with a full head of auburn hair and sparkling large yellow green eyes. We spent an interesting evening, the four of us with Prof. De Boer and his family. They were Hollanders who were interned by the Japanese, in Sumatra during the war, which they spent the in the infamous prison camps there. The next thing I remember was driving Edith, in by brothers Chevrolet to her parent's house in Edenvale. It was along evening. After that we became

close friends, which was then defined as going steady. Edith however had also, a number of ardent admirers, who frequently showered her with flowers and attention. I would not tolerate any of this, so if they wanted to invite Edith they would have to include me as well. And that's the truth. She often reminded me, how she had to ignore a beau one day, waiting for her in the foyer in the dorm, with an arm full of flowers, because I was waiting for her outside. Soon after, I met her mother who remained a friend for life. I remember Meg, as generous, vivacious woman still retaining the traces of her youthful beauty. Her father Ted was a more reserved, yet a very opinionated man of strong convictions. He was well read, liked playing the piano and could do almost anything well, except make a living. The family had to live in a large measure on Meg's earning as a secretary in a nearby Tuberculosis Sanitarium. Ted tried some wild hare business schemes such as, breeding rare Budges, or manufacturing shoe polish, never succeeding for any length of time, but he did have a phenomenal eye for property. When he and Meg were married, they bought a chicken farm of substantial size in Stanton, now the commercial center of Johannesburg's best suburb. When he sold the farm some years later, he just missed a phenomenal real estate boom, in that particular suburb. Had he waited just one year longer he would have become a rich man. I do not know if it was his usual business ineptitude or just bad karma for making money. He then bought a modest house in the outlying suburb of Edenvale and a non-productive farm on a spectacular property near Rustenburg, one hundred and twenty miles away from Johannesburg.

Edith was the oldest of the four Horn children who each in their own way were quite special. Johny was the least accomplished of the lot, being burdened by Asthma during his childhood and lack of appropriate home environment at that time. He struggled all his life working as a mechanic to support a handful of children some whom may not even been his. He spent a life of unmitigating hardships and penury. Teddy on the other hand became a great success in spite having left the school at the age of fourteen, to work on his own. By the age of twenty, he had a substantial workshop and eventually became a very successful proprietor of engineering works and man of property. Anne the youngest after following Edith at the Potchestroom High School for Girls became a teacher.

Medical School

For most part, I have enjoyed the years learning Medicine. However, six years is a long chunk of time. The grind in preparing for the annual examinations was very demanding, which created a recurrent anxiety. A failure could set one back six months to a year, or at best waste the summer vacations in preparation for a rewrite. Such a fate did befall a proportion of the class, each academic year. The results, which were posted weeks later, were awaited with nervous anticipation. There were no announcements as to when exactly we could expect the outcome, so to ward the end of each January, or some six weeks after the final papers and the orals, a crowd of us would gather on the steps of the main hall. Each day, we would anxiously scan the walls for the tally of the results. When they finally appeared, in a small print, on plain sheets of paper, we would scramble over each other to get in front, with beating hearts and sweaty palms. It was an indescribable relief to see one's name on the passing list. For some years after I finished Medical School, I had a recurrent nightmare reliving these moments. Only the final exam was the exception, when the results were announced promptly, on the same day. I still feel the thrill when one of my favorite professors, as he was leaving the examination hall, before the results were even known, said to me in passing "well George, you're doctor now".

The class consisted of one hundred and twenty students with the exception of the second year, when a bunch of attractive girls doing physio- or occupational therapy, joined us, for the anatomy lab. These were the days when female medical students were singularly unattractive. The demographics of the class were quite interesting. The class consisted of ten percent females, who one for one, were very bright, usually were much smarter and worked harder than the average male. They also usually did very well on the exams. Blacks, Coloreds and Indians were the other "minority" group of equal number. We were very proud of the fact that there was no social segregation while enjoying generally an easy interpersonal relation with one another. This was an anomaly at the time, as the rest of the country adhered strictly to the Laws of Apartheid. It was the internal policy of our University as a whole, to integrate the student body regardless of color. Despite the continued pressure, the faculty and student body successfully defied the government until the very end of apartheid.

The faculty at the Wits.Medical School, which was quite colorful, deserves some description. Raymond Dart the Prof. and Chair of Anatomy was one of the most renowned Physical Anthropologists of the Twentieth Century. His lectures on prehistoric Man were a hoot, but unforgettable. He was a small man, but broad shouldered, with a massive head, slightly stooped posture and with his rather long arms swinging, he would jump on the lecture counter to demonstrate the upright walk of an early humanoid, which we were convinced, he resembled. He was a man of great intellect and compassion, well deserving our respect and admiration. His disciple Phillip Tobias who succeeded him was also a respected anthropologist and a brilliant lecturer. I have fond memories of both these remarkable men. Dr. Arnold who managed the impossible, by making an anatomy lecture interesting. He would start with a simple drawing of bones, proceeding gradually to create with chokes of various color, layers of muscles with the corresponding nerves arteries and veins in perfect anatomic relation. Prof .Watt in Pharmacology was a character, both as a personality, as well as a teacher. Proud of his Scot ancestry, he would on occasion prance around the school in his kilt with all the trimmings. Early after the war, his class consisted predominately of Ex-service men. When one day they were particularly inattentive, many of whom, he noticed, were frankly sleeping, so to get their attention, he shot off a starting pistol. Some literally jumped out off their seats, creating a panic for a moment, thinking that they were in a combat again. In the third year, Bekker, the Prof. of Pathology, was a dour, demanding teacher, who while demonstrating a smoker's black lung, would commonly have a lit cigarette dangling from his lips. The Brothers Gilman run the Physiology department, the older being the Chair. They were politically liberal activists. Soon after I said my good byes to them, on my way to Canada, they left for Ghana, where Josef was appointed the Minister of Health by President Nkrumah. In the forth year I came to the attention of Prof. "Ozy" Heyns, the Chair of Obstetrics and Gynecology and I remained under his wing till I left South Africa. He was a brilliant man, if a touch inarticulate, with a thick Afrikaans accent. He had a very original and inventive mind, unfortunately lacked adequate resources for major scientific investigations, to follow his ideas. He was one of the pioneers of electronic fetal monitoring. He developed an experimental abdominal decompression chamber to aid women in labor. I was in many ways I was lucky to have him, as well some other members of his department,

such as Dr. van Dongen, as role models. One unforgettable character was Dr. Krige, a crusty old Afrikaner, a brilliant surgeon as he was as a teacher, despite his stubby fingers. Another, whose name escapes me, was a surgical gymnast who would tackle any patient no matter how complex, but with great bravura and skill. When ever I visited S.A. I made sure to see them. On several occasions I was there as a visiting Professor or had attended and presented papers at International Conferences which took place there. On the outside of the strictly full time academic faculty, Dr. Joel Cohen, was the best Gynecologic Surgeon I have ever witnessed. He was also a great teacher full of rich anecdotes and an ego to match. He would invite a small group of students in the final year, for good dinners, followed by intensive seminars in preparation for the exams. Later he became the Professor at a Tel-Aviv University. He visited with me on several occasions in NY where he lectured at Einstein and at Bronx Lebanon when I was in charge. He left me as a memento some of his surgical instruments which he designed and copies of the books he wrote. One of the most respected senior internists was "Mosy" Sussman whose claims to fame were numerous. He was a superb diagnostician, was the first to introduce Corticoid-steroid therapy to S.A. then a new, revolutionary medicine. He was the one, who diagnosed a Millary Tuberculosis in Mrs. Elenor Roosevelt, during one of his frequent visits to the USA. while others were baffled as to the cause her terminal illness. I was fortunate to have been assigned for my Medicine rotation to his ward. His other distinction was, that his wife was Helen Sussman. This very brave woman, who almost single handed, as member of S.A. Parliament, represented the liberal conscience of the country. For years, she had to face ridicule and hostility of the members, who were the government supporters of the Apartheid. Dr. Baynash, a senior Physician, whom I also counted as a social acquaintance and mentor, because by of my close friendship with his stepson, Sinclair Baylis. Writing about this brilliant but disturbed friend Sinclair, could by itself fill a chapter. Although he was not a medical student like us, having only got his B.A. at Wits, he attached himself to my circle of friends. We remained quite close, until he left the country some years later. He was a very needy person, often acting out inappropriately, but could be at times the most charming and generous friend. He was very creative. He helped us to present an avant-garde play in mime, for instance. He would amuse us with his satirical poems and often played the clown. We knew that there is something very wrong with him, but he would usually bounce back to an acceptable level of sanity. Things

were complicated by his over protective mother, who in an effort to assure some control, would frequently invite us to their lovely home for diners or a swim. She would even let him use her car, as long as, he was in our company. His behavior became more bizarre as time went on. Years later, I learned that he became a well-recognized published poet. Edith and I had the sad opportunity to visit him in a mental hospital outside London. He was a shadow of his former self, sans teeth, sans health, with out a shred if dignity left, but yet he still greeted us and with a warm smile of recognition. We understood that he might have been suffering from a life long Schizophrenia, which in retrospect would explain much of his earlier behavior. Anther of my friend was Simmy Friedman, a rather small, wiry, energetic fellow, an addicted gambler, with a perpetual crooked grin on his face, was another of my close pals. During the Patho-clinical sessions, when patient's illness was presented in an unfolding fashion and then correlated to the post-mortem findings, he would run up and down the isles of the lecture hall taking bets as to the final diagnosis. Every Saturday afternoon, he could be found at the race tract, when the horses were running. Girls were his other major sport. He on occasion discovered escorting three different student nurses, each one at the end of their tour of duty, in the same twenty four hour period. He too specialized in Obstetrics and Gynecology. Lorri and I had met him, on our recent visit to South Africa, on the occasion of my fiftieth class reunion. He was most hospitable and very gracious. Paul Klugman was another good friend, a tall handsome, personable man; an excellent golfer who tried to interest me in the sport to no avail. When I tried to get his address in Australia to resume contact after many years, I was discouraged from writing by Simy, because of Paul's depressed state of mind. The last and the closest of my friends in this group was Albert Kushlick whom I mentioned previously.

Of all the experiences at the Medical School, the most dramatic was the six weeks I had to spend as a junior intern at the Alexandria Township. Alexandra was one of several "locations" on the outskirts of Johannesburg, where the Black Africans, who worked in the city, called home. The others were Sophia Town and Baragwanath, the latter was the largest, the most infamous, which later became known as Soweto. Squeezed into the Alexandria Township's one square mile lived one hundred thousand people. Most lived in shacks made of corrugated tin with mud floors. Crime was rampant, especially Black on Black. The only

Medical care available was provided by a health station manned by Catholic Nuns with the assistance of Black nursing staff and paradoxically supervised by a couple of extremely left oriented doctors. Only recently I was reminded of the time I spent there, by a brilliant South African film "Tsotsi', based on a story by Athol Fugard. It starts with a scene of an older African man being stubbed to death with a sharpened bicycle wheel spike, through the heart, by a gang of juvenile thugs, known as Tsoties. It was reminiscent of my experience with one of my first patients, whom I encountered there, who was brought to the clinic with unexplained death. Eventually we discovered a pinpoint wound in the in the chest, which was explained to me as being probably caused by a sharpened bicycle wheel spike. It was then, as it is apparently still now, a favorite, silent, stealthy weapon favored by the juvenile gangs. Another incident that was somewhat emblematic of the African Natives' belief in the local voodoo lore was, when a boy of about sixteen, came in with a total nominal aphasia (loss of speech). The mother gave a history that for some reason the boy was cursed by the local Ungan (a witch doctor), as a punishment. Another student and I naively decided that it might be a form of hysteria, born out of fear. Without any farther consultation, we have embarked to try to get the boy to speak. We began to force him to repeat after us, such words as mama and other simple words in his native tongue. After what seamed like an endless time, he began at first to mouth and then to sound the words out. We were very pleased with the results of our simple therapeutic approach, but in retrospect, I wonder what emotional harm we might have done in the end. One other incident, which I vividly recall, was the night I was on duty, when a call came in, requesting help for women in labor. I was delegated to deliver this woman, but not being confident enough to fly solo, I have requested help. A black nurse familiar with the local alleys armed with a flashlight, carrying a labor pack accompanied me. I was less frightened for myself, as by wearing a white coat, was usually tantamount to a passport of protection. I was insecure that I would be unable to find the shack in the night. If the truth be told, I was more terrified by the prospect of delivering the pregnant woman by my lonely self. As we walked through the maze of darken hovels, I extracted a promise from the nurse that she will be there to help me with the delivery. When after several false trials, we have finally found her shack; a single candle lighted it. We found the woman alone in active labor. After making the appropriate preparations, which meant boiling water, while setting up for the delivery with some old newspapers, which we brought,

to serve as cover sheets. As the woman was about to deliver, she vomited all over the freshly starched white uniform of my nurse, to the latter great disgust. The nurse then bolted out of this single room shack to clean herself, while I was left, all alone at the critical time as the baby was delivering. That was the very moment I feared most. To compound my problems she took with her our bag containing instruments and medications. There I was on my knees on the mud floor, as the poor woman was lying on some excuse for a mattress. The baby, a healthy boy screaming loudly, was finally born. With not even a pair of scissors to cut the cord, I found eventually a rusty razor blade, but nothing to tie cord with, so I had to do it with a piece of old string. Eventually the nurse reappeared, although in a foul mood, and I corrected what ever I could, in an effort to provide some semblance of sterility.

I was also significantly involved in some extra-curricular activities within the school, such as becoming a member of the Student Medical Consul and the chairman of our Dramatic Society. The latter in particular allowed for participating meaningfully in staging an occasional play, which was usually presented to a wider audience, at the main campus of the university, once a year. The other responsibility which I have especially enjoyed was arranging for speakers of interest, to present at our monthly midday Cultural Society Lectures. Being separated from intellectual ferment by thousands of miles and having committed six years to study medicine, we felt very keenly the need to embrace especially any visitors from over-seas, who could offer cultural diversions. These lectures were open to all medical students, were well attended. The speakers could very from the visiting English gap-tooth comedian Terry Thomas to Alan Paten the author of "Cry the Beloved Country". I would frequently have also the privilege of introducing the speakers. I generally felt, that my life at the Medical School was not only fairly well rounded but often stimulating and fun.

After graduation those of us who were fortunate to get the internship in the Professorial firms at the Johannesburg General Hospital were given very comfortable accommodations at the Doctor's Residence and especially those who were married received good quarters. Life at the "Resdoc" as it was called for short, was short of nothing. It was a great opportunity for the young doctors, to socialize with one another. We were provided with free board. A dinning room furnished with tables with fine linen cloth and African servants in white

uniforms. Full housekeeping service, was also provided all this without any direct cost to us. We even had a daily portion of row filet mignon, for our Siamese cat Misiu.

This was also at the time when Edith and I got married. In the intervening years Edith first lived most of the year at the university residence and during vacations at her family. Home in Edenvaile. I first shared a flat with Ludwik and then I moved into a very spacious one bedroom apartment, in center of the city in an Art Deco stile building, so typical of Johannesburg. There we made friends with some of our neighbors. One was an elderly widow, Selma Kaufman, a German Refugee, whom Edith helped occasionally with sawing. In return Aunty Selma taught Edith some haute couture skills. In fact, Edith's wedding dress was designed and sawn by Ant Selma, who gave it to Edith, as a wedding gift. On one of our visit to Cape Town, where Mrs. Kaufman have retired, she gave us, at the age of ninety, a comprehensive tour of the city. Another very gifted artisan living in the same building was Eugon Gunther, then a recent German immigrant, a designer of modern jewelry of great originality and taste. Most of the jewelry that Edith brought from South Africa was made by him. Eventually he achieved a wider recognition by getting an award at a Venice Jewelry Exposition. When Edith and I visited with him later, in his newly designed Mexican type house in the suburbs, his garden contain the most comprehensive collections of cacti. By that time, he also became a respected collector/dealer of modern South African art.

If mention all these many, somewhat unrelated groups of people, it is because I would want indicate how privileged I was to meet so many of them on their on their way up, and not simply aiming at name-dropping. What intrigued me in particular, that in spite of its numerically small elite, South Africa was a cauldron of talent. The intellectual and artistic ferment was felt especially, in Johannesburg, where both the English and the Afrikaans theatre flourished. There were number of talented painters and sculptors, which began to include the native African artists. Writers from both language groups received worldwide recognition and acclaim. These intense artistic expressions, so far from centers of world culture at that time, might have been I suspect, in no small measure stimulated by the atmosphere political repression and unrest; perhaps not unlike in some way it might compared to that of the pre-revolutionary Russia.

The Pioneers

I had along pause in writing because of the winter holidays in the Death Valley in California, with Jill, John, and the children. Then a serious car accident delayed me even farther. My last chapter ended by introducing Edith and her immediate family, into my life, so perhaps it is fitting that that today, what would have been her 74th. Birthday I resume reminiscing about her. To remember Edith, one is immediately confronted by the memory of her extraordinary generosity, intellect, enthusiasm, creative energy, determination, but above all loyalty and love for her family and friends, which she possessed in great abundance. The dignity and courage with which conducted herself throughout the long months of her painful terminal illness, was another side of this extraordinary woman, who was my companion and wife for almost fifty years. Her prodigious energy and talents ranged from sewing to ditch digging, from an elegant turn of phrase to creative gardening, from the kitchen to the easel. Whatever the task or project at hand, she has invariably succeeded with great panache. Edith was truly not afraid, to tackle any task if she thought it was worth doing and doing it well. She was a good tennis player and was equally devoted to playing bridge. As an English High School teacher, she left a lasting impact on her students and earned a deep respect and admiration of her colleagues. At one time, early in our life in New Rochelle, she was instrumental in mounting a successful public resistance against placing an atomic power station, just off Glen Island. Her intrepid spirit, which never waned throughout her life, could probably be traced to her ancestors.

Edith's maternal ancestors by the name of Creoux came from Lausanne Switzerland probably in the 1870 ties. They were deeply religious Protestants missionaries tracing their family roots to the French Huguenots. The great grand Father Ernest Creaux co-founded a missionary hospital and an adjoining Leper colony, at Elem in northern Trans-Vaal, near the border of Southern Rhodesia (Zimbabwe). The hospital still exists and provides care for the Native People of the region, the Vendas. We visited there on our way to Edith's cousins, the other descendants of the Creoux. They owned some luscious farmland with orchards of avocados and macadamia nuts. One memorable late afternoon her cousin took us on bumpy

ride over the fields, without any road, to witness a sunset from a mountaintop. It was a beautiful sight, looking over the green hills and valleys, while enjoying a fine bottle of white wine.

Toward the end of his life the great grand father Erenest Creoux and his wife moved to Pretoria, where they lived next to Paul Kruger, *the president of the country and the hero of the Boer War. During that war, they were committed supporters of the resistance to the British. Etienne one of their sons who was Edith's Grand Father, settled northeast of Johannesburg, in a small industrial town of Midlleburg. His wife Blanche Volez, whom I had the privilege to meet, when she was already in her nineties, was a sage and a saintly person. She was lovingly addressed by all as "Gaminy". She came to South Africa in hope to be cured of Tuberculosis in its hot dry climate. At that time, the only hope for cure was rest and nutrition. Apparently, they had to wait seven years until they got married, by which time she was considered cured and not infectious any more. They had four children the oldest of whom was Margaret or Meg, who was Edith's mother.

Because of the World War II and the financial difficulties, when her father was in the army, her mother Meg had to work. Consequently, Edith spent a large part of her childhood in the care of her Grandparents. Their character and personalities left a major impact on her. From the Grand Mother she learned compassion, generosity and respect for people regardless of race or color. Although Edith was not pious, she acquired an encyclopedic knowledge of the bible, especially of the Old Testament, which was read aloud by her grandfather, each evening after dinner and on Sundays. Etienne Creoux at that time had exclusive rights to Coca-Cola and represented the Ford car company for the region. Despite this opportunity, he never over the years gained any the potential financial rewards. His strong religious believes against usury, prevented him to run a business on credit bases, essential and commonplace for any such enterprise. In contrast, Edith's paternal grandparents were staunch Catholics, especially Grand Mother Horn. She was a fierce, quick-tempered woman of small stature, with a head of flaming red hair in her youth. According to the family lore, she was not above horse whipping any of her five sons, when she thought a situation demanded castigation. When she learned that Edith was going out with me, having been told that I came from

Poland, she warned her that I would probably stab her with a knife one night. She was full of blind prejudice against any body that was not English. Edith thought that her grand mother might have been of Irish decent and even suspected that in the early years she might have been a chorus girl, because of the occasional tendency to erupt into a little dancing gig. Despite her dour personality, she did eventually warm up to me, when I helped looking after her varicose veins ulcers. There was however, a very special relation that Edith had with her Grand father George. She adored him from early childhood and remained his favorite grand child, until his death. George Horn came to Africa with the British Expeditionary Force under Kitchener's Command. After the Boer War, he worked for the South African Railways. During World War II, he and his sons opened a very successful engineering works near Johannesburg. His passion throughout his life was go into then still quite wild African "feld" to explore and hunt. He also imbued Edith and her father with love of gardening, being known throughout his community for his roses. Thus, Edith was born into families who were extremely religious Christians, but with an opposite creed. Politically there was a similar schism, in that that the Creouxs identified themselves with the Boer cause, while the Horns were committed to England, the Mother country. The religious and political differences between these two families were emblematic for the country as a whole. In the end, neither of her immediate families really benefited form the potential as pioneers, despite having arrived so early in that land of unlimited promise.

*Paul Kruger strangely enough was one of my childhood heroes. I received as gift an illustrated book on the Boer War for children. A particular incident in which Kruger amputated his injured thumb particularly stuck in my memory.

Family and Friends

Edith and I while still students, lead quite an interesting life in Johannesburg. She had some very good friends from her early school days in Portchestroom and then made many more while at Wits I too have enlarged my circle of friends both from the Medical School, as well as, from those who were my brother's acquaintances. In the earlier years I lived first in Bob's home, then together in a flat with Ludwik, but soon after his marriage to Dzizia, I had my on

apartment. There was quite a lively group of Polish immigrants, predominantly Jewish, who like us, with in a relatively short time, were well established. Bob and Audrey had their own group of friends but there was only a little of social mixing between them.

Among the Polish group, there were some fine people of interest. The first who come to mind were the Astons, Lucy and Adam. He was popular crooner (ala Bing Crosby) in pre-war Poland, but by now a shadow of his former self. Although still an elegant man, very much the Boulevardier, he was unable to resume his previous vocation. Lucy was a very warm, vibrant, beautiful, elegant woman, with a great personality and charm. She became a milliner to support the two of them, although according to Ludwik she has inherited a small fortune from her former lover in Argentina. Then there was Toncio, a beloved former Polish radio comedian, known for his regional accent and wit of Lwow, in the province of Galicia. He like many others, whom I mentioned here, would eventually leave South Africa for England. Once there, he married a woman from the Polish nobility and a doctor, who unfortunately died in subway accident. Their son became a well-known reporter for Reuters. Others worth mentioning was the family Cyprys. Although, both were lawyers, they were unable to practice in South Africa, yet they managed to thrive there, bringing up two daughters, one of whom was born during the war. I recall a most remarkable story of her survival as an infant. She was thrown out of a small window of a cattle car of a moving train, by her mother during transport on the way to the extermination camp. Somehow, Mrs. Cyprys managed to jump also off the train herself soon after. Although badly hurt, she somehow managed to find her infant daughter found at the local peasants. How and where they eventually survived, I do not remember. The Steinberg family, were the neighbors of Bob and Audrey in their first home in Parkhurst. He was a very intelligent, engaging man who was then the local director of General Electric. His wife was the sister- in-law of the famous miniature painter, Arthur Schick. Their daughter Edith, for whom I often baby set, later married a Scotch lawyer by the name of Rifkin, who at one time served a the British Foreign Minister in Mrs.Thatcher's conservative government. One of the most distinguished members of this small group of immigrants in Johannesburg, who were our friends, was Aaron Klug. He received the Nobel Price in Chemistry in 1982, while a professor at Cambridge and was given the Knighthood by the Queen. It is quite remarkable that I should have known from that small community in

my youth, two future Nobel Prize winners. The other was a colleague from the Medical School years. Sidney Brenner received the award for Molecular Biology in 2002, also while also, a professor at Cambridge.

While at Wits. Edith became friendly with two of her English Professors, Zoë and Harry Girling and they in turn introduced us to Sidney and Felicia Kentridge. This led to a life long friendships with both families that enriched our lives so much. The Girlings moved to Toronto, so we had the opportunity to visit one another and attend some of the children's weddings. Unfortunately, they both died a few years ago. The Kentridges, both lawyers remained in South Africa for many years after we left. They both were deeply involved in advocating for the civil and legal rights for the Black Africans. Sidney, was, leading the legal team that successfully challenged the notorious South African Police, accused of excessive brutality, in the case of Steven Biko, a Black activist, who died in their detention. That was a human rights case, which reverberated though the world and was one of the seminal events, which brought the injustice of Apartheid, into to the consciousness of the world. While Sidney was certainly interacting with the nascent Black freedom movement, he managed to avoid being banned outright, by the Government. Thus over the years he became to be recognized for his courage to face and battle, a very hostile, pathologic legal system of South Africa in the days of Apartheid. Later, he also became a renowned civil layer of international fame. It is remarkable that as non-academician he was a visiting Professor at the Harvard Law School. On another occasion he was awarded the Order of Coif by the Law School of the University of Pennsylvania, as well as, being honored by the New York Bar. I only know of these few outstanding recognitions, as I was privileged to attend some of these events. His wife Felicia, while bringing up four children, was also very active in an organization making legal services available to poor Black population. She was a most attractive, woman, an epitome of culture and elegance. It was always a great pleasure to visit the Kentridges in their homes; being in Johannesburg or London. The last time I saw them was by shear coincidence on the day of their fiftieth wedding anniversary, which the three of us celebrated by going to a charming Italian restaurant. That was also an opportunity to congratulate Sidney for being recently knighted by the Queen.

The impact that the Kentridge family made, extends in particular to their son William, who is by now is a recognized multimedia artist of world fame. My children and I have some of his etchings. One in particular, which reflects on his visit to New York City, when early in his career he tried, with Edith's help, get to one of the local galleries, he inscribed to her. He was met with a total rejection at that time. Now his work is shown in one of the most respected galleries of modern art here. He exhibited at the Guggenheim, the MOMA and the Metropolitan. In every one of these museums, he had one man shows and that is only in New York City. The last time Lorri and I went to one the openings, he reminded me that at the age of fourteen, he was given his first seal-hair paintbrush by Edith. From the very beginning, she had unfailing belief in his talent, as a major artist.

One other South African couple whom I met in my early days at the university and with whom Edith and I remained lifelong friends, are the Benfields, Thora, Desmond and their children. Fortunately our lives ran on parallel tracts, as they too immigrated to Canada. Then for a time, when Desmond was the Ontario trade representative here, they lived in New York. They eventually settled back in Toronto. We try to see each other on every occasion, when they visit their children here, who settled and thrived in the USA. Desmond became an aficionado of my herring and Vodka parties, so that is another incentive for a get together.

While Edith and I were still at the university, both my brothers began to settle down. At first, it was Bob and Audrey who moved from their first house to a very lovely home and garden at a prime location in the Zoo Lake area. After the birth of Robert, they had three more children James and the twins Barbara and Peter. Edith and I were always welcomed in their home. We were delighted at any opportunity, to either baby sit or to take the older boys for outings. Celebrating X-mass with them was an annual event, which invariably took place on a very hot December day, with the usual excess of food and drink. It was made particularly festive, by the child like delight and happiness of the African servants. It was the time of "X-mass Box", mandatory gifts for the servants from the "Master and Madam". Especially in the early days when alcoholic drinks were illegal for the Blacks, they would use such festive occasions, as an opportunity to get completely soused by drinking what ever was left in the

glasses and pinching a bottle or two on the side. Needless to say, that the carnage on the roads at X-mass and New Year was fearsome in South Africa.

It was an interesting house in many ways, as Audrey with a good taste created an elegant, yet comfortable home. The Sunday dinners there were memorable as much for their protocol of manners, as it was for the classic English cooking, which was actually, outstandingly good Bob was an inveterate collector of short focus and a hungry eye. When he decided that he will grow roses he would make certain that he would have, as many varieties as, it was possible to grow, even at the expense of the rest of the garden. When his fancy turned to tropical fish, he literarily filled the garage wall to wall with fish tanks. At one time, he showed great interest in Georgian silver and antique furniture, which led to his frequenting auction sales. However, I must say, that he had a good eye, excellent taste, coupled with great enthusiasm. He did have one sustained interest from his early youth, which was, stamp collecting. Eventually he won an international prize for his complete collection of postage stamps of the Seychelles Islands. Later in life, while in England he amassed together with his son Robert, a comprehensive collection of Chinese Snuff Bottles, which they described and presented in a beautifully illustrated book. His son Robert is now the preeminent world authority and a dealer in snuff bottles and other Chinese artifacts.

Ludwik in the mean time, on one of his travel to Europe, stopped on the way in Israel where among our friend from Radomsko, he found the family Kreindler. You may recall that it was Mr. Kreindler who left with us, on the first day of the war, in an effort to escape the invading Germans. He rejoined his family in the Russian occupied zone, from where they were transported to Siberia. Having survived the war under severe hardships there, they went back to Poland and eventually settled in Israel. Their older daughter Stefa studied medicine, while Dzidia did radiology. It must have been a love at first sight, because as soon after, Dzidia came to South Africa where they were married. Eventually they moved from the apartment, which I shared with them, to a very nice house in the northern suburbs. No much later their daughter Jane was born. For me it was always a great pleasure to visit there, as Dzidzia became a fabulous cook. To this day I look especially forwards to my visits to London, not only be with them, but to enjoy once more, sitting around their table at a remarkable meal.

After some years in Johannesburg the family was once more enlarged, by the arrival from England of Audrey's Mother. Bee (Patricia) Balleny, who must have been at least in her sixties at the time, was a widow, to who attribute of "merry" was never more fitting. This charming, ageless, beautiful woman, yet good and kind, soon found herself adored by all who met her. She was just a fun person to be with, regardless of one's age. It was in contrast to her daughter, who in her younger years was rather a prim and proper person. Audrey was very much conscious of her English origins, with a touch imperial hauteur, so commonly found among the transplanted British. Soon after her arrival in South Africa, Bee took up for a friend, a lapsed Jesuit, a man younger than she was. He was an intelligent, erudite interesting man but with a weakness for a bottle. Both Edith and I enjoyed their company very much.

In our early Johannesburg days, before he went back to England Audrey's brother Jack, an officer in the British Merchant Marine, was also part of our immediate circle, for a short time. We became quite good friends despite our difference in age. It was he in fact, who very patiently taught me how to drive a car, which in the days of stick shift was very challenging; which as it certainly it was for me. He was very entertaining fellow. It was fun listening to him, recalling his seadog days, having sailed the seven seas. He was a good man and I was sorry to have lost touch with him.

For me it was very gratifying and important to have my close family near by and be embraced by them. I must say that the same goes for Edith's family, where I also always felt at home. That was so even during our rather four year long courtship. Her mother Meg and I became close friends. She was unfailingly welcoming and kind, as were most of the members of her immediate and extended family.

Life in South Africa had other enormous advantages. There were so many beautiful and interesting places to see and visit. I took every opportunity, during vacations to travel. Even before I met Edith, I had some memorable trips. A July vacation in Durban with its great beaches on the Indian Ocean, where despite the winter season the weather was warm, while Johannesburg was freezing, once the sun went down. Very popular winter resort, as well as metropolitan city at that time, it had great hotels with very good food. Because of the large, originally imported population of "coolies" to labor as indentured workers in the sugar cane fields, Durban was steeped in East Indian sub-culture with a memorable oriental market, known especially for it exotic spices. A major event at that time was the July horse races there, which spiked a general national interest. No trip to Durban was complete, without having a picture taken in a colorful rickshaw being pulled by powerful Zulu. He wore an exaggerated native dress, with a huge, elaborately decorated headgear. The Natal province where the Zulu homeland was situated, before the English settlers arrived there in 1820,was known as the Valley of the Thousand Hills. The Zulu Nation is one of the one of the most prominent tribal groups in South Africa. The Natal province was distinctly different at that time, as there was no discernable Afrikaner impact on the predominantly English culture, among the white population, as opposed to the rest of the country.

Visiting Cape Town was always a special treat as long as one avoided the winter when the rain was frequent and the wind strong enough to lift a man, three feet high. Summer on the Muzenberg Beach, on the Indian Ocean with the predictable, champagne like frothy surf and the surrounding hills, was delightful. On one such vacation in Cape Town, I met with a group of my Johannesburg friends and we have literally painted the town red. As medical students, we had access to the Groot Schuur hospital, so we were never short of dates with the young nurses. At that time I stayed with family friends. Lola Pozwolski was a fabulous cook, but she only entertained in her house, two or three times a year, but when she did, she did it in stile. She prided herself that she never took less than three days, to prepare a special dinner. I was lucky to be in their house on one such occasion. It was there when I tasted Beef

Wellington for the first time, during a truly memorable dinner. It was also during the same visit to Cape Town, when a group of us set on the veranda of a hotel in Sea Point, drinking the "Kilimanjaro" cocktails. I was never sure whether indeed it was the real name of the drink or Sinclair Baylis' imaginary invention. At any rate, it consisted of tomato juice, a jigger of sherry, a splash of bitters and some pepper and it tasted just right. What a sight it was to sit high above shore, watching the Cape Rollers, as the rough waters of the cold Atlantic Ocean are known. To think that only a few miles away, just on the other side of the Cape, is the pacific, warm Indian Ocean. South Africa never failed to amaze with its so many faceted contrasts in nature, as in people.

When I became aware that there are also significant mountain ranges in South Africa, I was instantaneously intrigued by a possibility of a trip to Drakensberg. When a friend offered me a lift there, on his way to Durban, I accepted eagerly. Although the beauty and majesty of the mountain was undeniably, that particular holiday turned up to be a dud. The accommodations were dreadful, the company even worse and I was bitterly cold all the time, for which I was not properly prepared.

One of the memorable holidays was a leisurely trip to the Kruger National Park and Lorenzo Marquez in Mozambique, in the Portuguese East Africa, with Edith and her Mother Meg. To be in this great natural reserve, in those days when we stayed in very simple camps with correspondingly modest accommodations, such as the rather primitive "Rondavels" (a round hut with a thatched roof) was great fun, until we heard an elephant stomping in the night near by. We cooked the food outside on a few sticks of dry wood, with the monkeys all around. The cool nights with starry skies dominated by the Southern Cross, was a sight to see. During the nature drives, either in the morning or the late afternoon, we would never tire of spotting the great variety of wild life, so dramatic in their natural habitat.

The visit to Lorenzo Marquez was also most rewarding, in another way. It was an old colonial town, with the characteristic Portuguese architecture, spread along the Indian Ocean. In a teasing contrast, there was also number of buildings in strikingly modern stile. The whole tenor of the town was so different from the Dutch and English influence in South

Africa. The most dramatic difference, which was so striking for us, was the absence of Apartheid. The discrimination if there was any, was economic rather than social or political. Food too was so different from what we were used to eat at home. One special food experience was a meal in a very simple restaurant, which stood on stilts in the middle of the bay. We arrived there on barge, among sacks of flower, chickens and other assorted goods. We were served shrimp soup with Piri Piri, a strong spice specific to that part of the world. This was followed by an enormous bowl prawns with their heads on. It was a special treat to eat the fresh shellfish, which was just collected about hour before from the nearby waters. What added to the pleasure of this trip was the warm welcome we were given by the natives, both Black and White alike wherever we went.

Nothing however comes even close, to my deep emotional attachment and great personal pleasure, which I derived from visiting "The Farm" otherwise known as Ted's Folly. From the very first moment, I laid eyes on it, I was enchanted by its unique surroundings. It was as if I came upon my own private Shangri La. It lay in a flat ravine fronted on one side by a high ridge of reddish rock not unlike the palisades along the Hudson River and almost equally high. In the late afternoon sunset, it was brilliantly lit by an orange glow. A narrow river ran below the cliffs shaded by a row of willows. The rest of the valley was given over to well kept citrus farm. The scent of the orange blossoms wafting on gentle breeze and the imposing quiet, except for the ever present birds' songs, added to this enchanting atmosphere. When Edith brought me there for the first time, the farmhouse, if one could call this ram-shackled place that, had only a tin roof, brown brick walls and windows with chicken wire, for panes. Mud floors and a loosely closing door made of raw wooden planks, with neither indoor kitchen nor pluming provided, little comfort at the time but a lot of character. The food was cooked outside on a single ring, iron stove, and one item at the time. Yet, I never enjoyed eggs and bacon more, than upon our arrival there, for the very first time. The smell of the cooking bacon in the pure country air, after an arduous car journey, over rough country roads, was beguiling. One of the more terrifying things about the place was the fear of snakes. On the road to the farm that day, I run over a Mamba, a very dangerous African poisonous snake. I earned Edith's wroth because she heard that a snake could squeeze through an opening for the clutch pedal. The local snake lore was full such stories

and Edith, who having had a first hand experience of snakes on the farm, was very nervous. Her other anxiety which I foolishly, did not share at that time, concerned the insecurity of an isolated, unprotected dwelling, where the next neighbor lived miles away. Her particular phobia however, were the enormous African moths, which appeared in great numbers in the evenings, the minute any source of light was brought into a dark room. There was no electricity at that time, so the kerosene lamps added another layer of charm to the place, and a flashlight was an absolute necessity. As we visited the place over the years, which I never missed, even on our occasional trips from America, the farm underwent many improvements. Some fine houses were built, first for the older Horns, then for Teddy and Ann. One year when we arrived with Jillian and John, when they were still quite young, we had a delightful stay there. Ted Horn built a spectacular terraced vegetable garden, with raised beds enclosed by bricks. What a wonderful time the children had with a new litter of puppies to play with. There was a great variety of domesticated fowl roaming an around; also a cow or two and even some pigs. The baboons would often try to sneak into the garden or steal oranges from the orchard. To scare them off one day, Meg accidentally shot one from a long distance, which became a legend among the native workers, who rewarded her at that time, with a deeply felt "wow Missis"! However, this too had to end when Ann and her family left for Ireland and Teddy who owed the farm, eventually sold it. It did leave me however, with a deeply nostalgic memory of the especially delightful time, which I enjoyed there.

Our life in Johannesburg in contrast, both before and after we were married, was intensely social. The cinema, theatre, nightclub dancing, dinner parties or just hanging out with family or friends, crowded our life. The fantastic climate of Johannesburg lend itself to the life outdoors. Entertaining around the swimming pool or at the tennis court was common in this most generously hospitable community. How charming were the Garden Parties, where the girls in their wide brimmed hats, in bright summer dresses enlivened the scene. As I said before, for me, this was the "Land of the Lotus Eaters."

On the other hand, the socio-political situation became progressively more oppressive. The disparity of our life in contrast to the great majority of the Native Black population became a daily dilemma, without any equitable solution on the horizon. No matter how liberal one

might be, by the shear fact of living there as a White person, one benefited from the unequal advantage. The other dilemma was the obvious anxiety of the potential bloody conflict, should a day of reckoning ever arrive. I became obsessed with the lack of long-term hope for the Country and our future fate. My war experience was obviously a sensitizing factor in my being nervous, not to be once again compelled to" escape my home, on the last train from a beleaguered city". The constant pressure to leave South Africa from the very onset paradoxically came not from me, but from Edith. It was She who felt strongly, that we had no moral right to continue to live there, under these conditions. I on the other hand, considered South Africa a paradise, especially so in the early years there. As time went by, I became aware that my brother Ludwik, also became restless. It was at his daughter's Jane third birthday party, that a Mrs..Cherny, our devoted secretary, mentioned this to me. The next day I have asked Ludwik and Bob to meet with me at a local café to discuss the situation. I indicated that I am now at crossroad in my career, where I need farther education, if I were to specialize. This meant going to Great Britain for the final certification, in which case Edith and I might decide to stay there. I did indicate however, my reservation of living in Europe again, so the only realistic choices were either America or Canada. At that time, the U.S.A. was embroiled in the Communist paranoia as it was exemplified by the Un-American Senate hearings and by Senator Joseph McCarthy and his cabal. Canada looked attractive especially in that Ludwik has spent some time there so he had a first hand experience. I felt strongly that this was now a timely opportunity for Edith and me to leave for good. I urged my brothers, that they should also consider such choices. More over, made it clear that I very much hoped, that we would reassemble in a country of mutual choice. Getting the permanent Canadian visas at that time when its government encouraged new immigration was far easier and faster than trying to get to the States. I must say that Canada was a clearly, at least to me, the more attractive proposition. This was based, however, on a very naïve, very limited knowledge of the general conditions there, nor did I have any realistic expectations of what may lay ahead. As luck would have it, a help came from an unexpected source. A week or so after the family council, I was seating at lunch with a group colleagues, when the conversation turned to discussion concerning future career plans. Peter Beardall, a young intern, whom I hardly knew at that time, mentioned that he has plans to do his training in Obstetrics and Gynecology, at the McGill Medical School teaching hospital, in Montreal. He

elaborated farther that this was made possible because of an influential senior member of the department was his wife's uncle, a Dr. Thomas Primrose. As Peter was only at the beginning of his internship, he would not be going there for at least a year or more. On hearing of his plans I blithely declared that I too plan to immigrate to Canada. Then I had a second thought and asked Peter if he would be so kind as to inquire, if by any chance there might be a position in their program for me. By now, I had two and a half years of postgraduate training under my belt, of which eighteen months consisted of Obstetrics and Gynecology. In a case where ignorance was bliss, I had no concept of the stellar, worldwide reputation, of the McGill University. Were I to face the reality of the proposition, I would not have had the gumption to make such an inquiry. In fact, when to my attar delight a letter arrived stating that they do in fact have an opening, it was only then I gradually realized what an extraordinary opportunity this was. Apparently, a second year resident broke her legs in a skiing accident so severely, that she would be unable to resume her position in the foreseeable future. The letter also requested documentation of my training and letters of recommendation. Professor Heyns, although doubtful of a successful outcome, wrote a very generous letter of support, as did his other colleagues. Three weeks later, I was offered a second year residency position, but for one academic year only. It was because of pyramidal nature of their program, they could not guarantee an automatic promotion to the position of a chief resident. Another caveat was that I must assume the position, not later, than by the end of August of that year. I enthusiastically accepted their proposal and proceeded urgently, to obtain a permanent Canadian entry visa for Edith and myself. It was however by now, an early April of 1957. To compound my problems I became severely ill with a rare form of Mononucleosis, which not only necessitated prolonged hospitalization but also blood transfusions. To my great relief it all ended well and in good time. Edith and I left South Africa on the 30th of June 1957.

P.S.

I have spent eleven most wonderful years in this land of such beauty. I imbibed of its generosity and hospitality. I witnessed its tragic socio-political complexities. If one can use the word, love to describe one's emotional attachment and a gratitude to a country, then

indeed a love it was. It was a love at first sight and this emotional attachment still lingers to this day.

I would be amiss, if would not mention once again, that whatever I managed to achieve would be unattainable, with out the sustained and unstinting emotional and financial support of Ludwik and Bob. They acted in loco parentis for so many years and cared deeply for my welfare. They have my undying gratitude.

O Canada!

The Grand Tour

When all of the most important arrangements were in place for our new life, I turned my attention to less weighty matters. I thought that this enormous journey we were contemplating should perhaps include a tour of some parts of Europe, as this might be the last opportunity for an extended visit which, our professional responsibilities may prevent us, to do so in the future. I was particularly excited by the prospect of showing Edith the world. After a great farewell party given by Ludwik and Dzizia on a freezing June evening, we left the next day on an Alitalia propeller driven airplane, from the Jan Smuts Airport, Edith ebullient, and I in tears. I felt enormously sad at that moment leaving behind both our families, whose warm embrace I so appreciated. I was also full of anxiety despite my earlier resolve and enthusiasm, to be once more facing an unknown future.

In those days it was a long flight over the eastern Africa, interrupted for refueling, a number of times, until finally on a clear morning the southern coast of Greece came into our sights. Athens was a very gratifying experience. I was very moved when I saw from afar, the Parthenon for the first time. I was struck by the import that the beginning of western civilization was embodied in these ancient monumental ruins. We engaged a professor of history from the local university, to be our guide in exploring historic Athens. She however could only converse with us either in French or in German. So throughout the day Edith had to translate to me the French descriptions and I in turn did the same when the guide spoke to me in German. After we climbed the Parthenon, we had the whole place to ourselves, there were so few tourists at that time in Greece. The place was in moderate disarray, in contrast to when I had an opportunity to visit again many years later, when in it was somewhat restored, but also crowded with tourists.

From there, we proceeded to Italy where we stayed in Rome, Naples and Capri. We dropped plans to visit Florence because of a severe heat wave there, which apparently caused a number of deaths, according to newspaper accounts. Rome in July was also beastly hot and the ever-present noise of the Vespas made for a very restless sleep. We could only venture

out in the late afternoon. We stayed in a modest pension near the Via Nationale. It took me a while to realize that the "pronto" was a telephone greeting and not a countenance to be fast. I recall with great pleasure a late afternoon visit to the Forum Romanum, we were so enchanted by the experience, that we failed to leave before closing. At that time, the area was fenced off only with a wire mesh. Gradually we became aware, that we were there all alone except for the company of some feral cats. Fortunately the fence did not present a major obstacle. We did the sightseeing of the usual tourist attractions, but one visit, which stood out, was the day we spent at the sulfur baths, on the way to Hadrian's Villa. We bathed in cascading warm sulfur stream smelling strongly of rotten eggs. We then proceeded to the Villa D'este with its unforgettable garden of a hundred fountains with a beautiful view of the Campania. The rest of the afternoon was spent at the rather impressive Hadrian villa, which we followed by visiting a neighboring old Etruscan town. The visit to Naples was somewhat of a disappointment, but the stay in Sorrento was memorable. It was made especially so, by an invitation to visit the private apartment of the hotel owner. We were waiting for a cab at the gates of the hotel, to take us to the harbor, for a trip to Capri. It was already uncomfortably hot in the blazing sun, when an elegant man introduced himself as the manager of the hotel offering to arrange for the taxi, while we could wait in his apartment. We accepted the invitation with some hesitation, but we were amply rewarded. The hotel stood high over the cliffs facing the Mediterranean with a view of Vesuvius across the bay. The apartment we were taken to was in the lowest part of the hotel, which was built on what originally was an old cloister. To our surprise we entered a cavernous, somewhat dark room, lined with mahogany bookcases on one side, with a line of heavily curtained windows facing it. The floor was carpeted with oriental rugs and there was a grand piano in one corner. It appeared that the owner was an avid collector of first additions of Tasso's "Jerusalem" published over the years, in different languages. Most of the bookcases were devoted to this extra ordinary collection. We admitted with chagrin to our lack of awareness of its contents or the author. This was patiently explained to us while we had tea on a little balcony, high above the water's edge. It was also there, he told us is, where he breakfasts each morning with his mistress. The visit ended by him playing Chopin's etudes for us. This unexpected experience left a charming, life long memory.

When we finally got on to the boat to Capri, in what was a rickety old sail boat with a motor, uncomfortably crowded with about ten passengers. On the boat with us was a very friendly pair of Americans. He was a professor of Psychology at a college in Rutherford New Jersey. He told us that he was a former Protestant minister and a victim of Polio. He was large bulky man, who moved with difficulty because of the iron braces on both legs. She in contrast was a small, delicate woman with a lovely gentle face and manners. Both were older than we were, but they were extraordinarily friendly, open and charming. It was one of those instant friendships, which were to last for ever. There and then they invited us to visit, if we ever come to the States. We did that when Jillian was six weeks old and stayed with them in Rutherford. When we later moved to New Rochelle they and Adam Novak helped us buying our first house, by lending the down payment money, without any security. After Mary died from ovarian cancer, Bill Hunter remarried a lapsed Catholic nun, who was a spitting image in all respects, of his former wife. They moved to Chicago where eventually we lost contact. It was a great privilege and of an enormous intellectual benefit for us, to have known and been befriended by the Hunters. The most lasting memories of Capri, was the visit to Axel Munth's house and a severe gastro-enteritis as a result of drinking the local water.

On the way to Switzerland we stopped in Milan where we took a local train to a small town on the southern shore of Laggo Majore. There we boarded a ferry to Locarno. We were lucky to have a good weather, so this rather longish sail was most pleasant and quite spectacular, with mountains arising from both shores of this rather narrow lake. We made plans to visit with Edith's Great Aunt Olga Valey at her home in Locarno, a sleepy little city on the northeastern corner of the lake. Its claim to fame was that some major treaty was signed there, after World War One. We had no exact address except for the name of her cottage was Les Hisrondelle. Thinking that it might not be too far from the ferry station, we started walking, lugging our enormous luggage up the rather steep streets, as we were directed. The cottage proved much farther and higher in town that we anticipated, but the effort was awarded by a very warm welcome. Aunt Violette by then was probably in her eighties. She was small and thin little woman, not unlike a sparrow, after which she named her cottage in French. We left our suitcase in the entrance hall as both Edith and I were thoroughly exhausted, only to have found them later, to our surprise already in our rooms, on the third

floor. This little old, seemingly frail woman, unbeknownst to us, brought them there herself. We spent a few charming days there, exploring the local countryside, had picnics in the fresh mountain air and generally hiked a lot. When from the occasional visit to the town proper, I would take a taxi to avoid the long climb back, I was chided by Aunt Violette for wasting my money. She was a most generous and charming hostess. Although she was a spinster, who came from the poor side of Edith's Grandmother's family, the house belonged to her. It was given to her as a reward for keeping and protecting an escaped Italian Jewish family there, during the latter part of the war.

We also visited with the Creoux, part of the family in Lausanne, but it was less rewarding. We also spent some time in Bern and Geneva. While waiting for a ride to Grenoble on a sleepy Sunday afternoon in cramped confines of a small bus station consisting of single room, a well dressed woman entered, requesting help from the one only attendant. He was still recovering of what must have been a very satisfying Sunday dinner, accompanied probably by a generous amount of wine. He was slow to rise, but when he noticed the rather large volume of the woman's luggage outside, he came back in, shaking his head in disgust while mattering under his breath for all to hear "baggage! baggage monumental!!!. Of the few of us in the room, none could refrain from laughter, except the American women, whose luggage it was. The reason for our visit to Grenoble, was to meet my French cousin Richard and his family. He was a son of my father's brother Solomon, previously mentioned in a rather less than complimentary portrayal. Richard was in France before the war to study dentistry, and then when the Germans occupied that part of the country he escaped to Switzerland. By the time we met, he was married to Marie, they had two children Nelly and Bernard, and had a well established dental practice in town. Having received a very warm welcome, we stayed a while exploring the surrounding countryside which is spectacular, particularly Chamonix. A ride in cable car up the Ille de Medie, suspended on stupendously long cables, up the top of this huge cold mountain, to view the Mont Blanc, was terrifying. But it was not as terrifying as riding in four seat prewar Renault, six of us squeezed to the max, while Richard was careering round the S curves of the Alpine road, with total abandon. Another memorable day was spent hiking to the Monastery of the Monks responsible for the Chartreuse liqueur. On the way there, to great delight, we gathered wild strawberries in the

woods, a great delicacy, which we ate at a mountain auberge, after a wonderful meal of fresh trout from the local stream.

Paris was our next destination, but here I was a little more at home because of my previous stay there, so I was able to guide Edith to points of interest. We stayed on the Left Bank, walked our feet of to point off bleeding, but what fun and privilege, it was to explore this great city. From there, as I mentioned before, we flew a helicopter to Bruxelle, to visit my aunt Erna and her sons. Our final European destination was the great city of London where we spent the remainder of our trip. We lived with our friends the Poseys and really had the opportunity for a leisurely but thorough look at the many remarkable historical sites and its many cultural institutions. We left England with a great anticipation of what might await us next.

The Warm Welcome and Cold Winters

Flying across the Atlantic in 1957 was more cumbersome than it is today, as it involved a refueling stop in Gander, Newfoundland. The commercial jet planes were yet to be introduced on a large scale. There was however, an earlier attempt by the British, ended in tragic failure, after several in-air disasters of the first Jetliner, the Comet, which apparently due to a metal fatigue. The Comet was a truly beautiful aircraft, elegantly designed, with the two jet engines seamlessly integrated, into its thin, slightly backswung wings. I saw it in a demonstration flight over Johannesburg in the early fifties.

We arrived in New York at Idlewild airport, (it was later named John.F. Kennedy) at the end of August, on a bright sunny morning. The arrival area was housed in a rather unattractive temporary building. My first quest was to contact telephonically my childhood friend, Bronka Novak. This lead to my first "Greener" experience on the shores of America. I needed a dime for the phone, when handed one, I gave in exchange a nickel and demanded another dime, to the disgust of the man helping me. As the nickel was a larger coin than the dime, not being familiar with the USA money, to my chagrin I assumed that it was worth twice as much. On the drive from the airport, it was quite thrilling to spot the imposing

Empire State Building within the panorama of Manhattan. We spent a few days exploring the city while staying in a fleabag of a hotel on Time Square. We did not find New York particularly enchanting, at that time.

We flew into Montreal in the early evening but with all the immigration procedures, we did not get to the hotel until well after 11 PM. While filling out the necessary documents at the airport, Edith was asked what kind of work she was seeking. When she responded that she very much hoped to find a teaching position, the immigration officer assured her enthusiastically, that she will have no problem getting a job, as Canada was so short of teachers, that now they even let the Jews teach. When we finally reached our hotel tired and hungry, the dining room was already closed by then. All the room service was able to provide us with, were some very dry ham sandwiches. I refused to have this rather inauspicious arrival to Montreal dampened my enthusiasm, so we ordered a bottle of Champagne to toast our new life.

We were received very warmly at the Royal Victoria Hospital, which was the clinical teaching center for the McGill Medical School, by its director and by the head of the O/G residency program, Dr. Primrose. I was to start almost immediately, while Edith through the kind services of Dr. Primrose was given appointment at a High School, teaching English. We settled quite quickly into our corresponding work routines. My work was rather brutal, because of the night call, every second day. Edith taught at school in the Town of Mount Royal, an upper end suburb of Montreal. She soon found us a very nice apartment, just off Cote de Neige, half way between her school and the hospital. Not having a car, public transportation was the only option, which in the harsh Montreal winter was a serious handicap. When the temperature dropped to ten below, which was not that unusual, hardly any protection was adequate. The cold was particularly penetrating because of the very high humidity, as Montreal is an island in the great St. Laurence River. Summers were very short, almost equally uncomfortable due also to the high humidity. The spring and fall were short, but the spectacular autumn in the Laurentian Mountains was for me, the seventh wonder of the world.

My co-residents Dennis Pollan and Peter Beck could not be nicer or more helpful and supportive. Of the two chief residents, one was a harsh, somewhat bitter man, while the other was a rather charming easy going Scot, with a thick brogue. I continued to be in contact with him, as Harry Manderson settled in Bermuda, where we visited with him on our trip there. He in turn came to New York a few times. On one such visit he came to our department wearing Bermuda shorts, so before I took him around the hospital, we gave him the standard white doctor's coat to wear. I could not understand why people were giving us amused glances as we were walking through the various wards, until I gave Harry a good look over. By wearing the long coat over the shorts, it appeared that he had left his trousers at home.

I felt very invigorated by the general tenor of the Medical Center, which even then was on the leading edge of many new developments in Medicine. Curare, a paralyzing agent to facilitate general anesthesia was developed in Montreal. One of our anesthesiologist was one of the pioneers and an authority on the epidural approach. In fact, I was doing total abdominal hysterectomies on patients under the epidural anesthesia, which at the time was a total novelty. In our department Dr. Latoure, was a leading light in gynecologic oncology and an early expert in the prevention and treatment of cervical cancer. The Ayred spatula, commonly use in obtaining a Pap smear throughout the world, was developed here. The department of Surgery was already doing successful kidney transplants. The coronary by pass by using the mammary artery was developed there. The Montreal Neurological Institute pioneered the mapping of the brain and had world-renowned neurosurgeons on their staff. The psychiatric department in the Allen Pavilion was already experimenting then, with the use of psychotropic drugs. They were also studying the effects of prolongation and depravation of sleep. It was suspected later, that these studies might have been supported with the CIA money; echo of the truth serum etc.? Other distinguished work was being done in endocrinology, radiation therapy and neonatology. The Montreal Children's Hospital became the nursery for a number of distinguished future chairs of pediatrics in the U.S.A. All this pioneering work was already going on in 1957. No wonder I was excited and grateful to able to learn medicine in such an exciting milieu.

The Royal Victoria Hospital was an imposing grouping of granite buildings, about four stories high. It was at the very end of the business center of the city, high on the hill, resting against the top of Mount Royal, a park and dominant feature of the town. Immediately below the hospital, build on a slope, was the vast campus of McGill University. Getting there by foot invariably required some huffing and puffing. Getting there by car was not a joy either, unless one was familiar with the one-way streets and had reserved parking. Driving a car there, greatly compounded during the endless winter. I often gazed through the windows of the hospital, on bitter cold mornings, looking over the roofs of the city; with the plumes of smoke rising form the chimneys, straight and high into the frigid air, and wondered what the future might hold.

On my first day at work, I was greeted and instructed by the vice chairman of the department, Paul Latour. He was respected by all as a brilliant teacher, surgeon and investigator who was one of the earlier gynecologic oncologists in the field. He was a somewhat small, moved fast, was rather stern in his manner, was always fair, but he did not suffer fools gladly. He was a bit of a anomaly, because he was a French Canadian of Protestant persuasion. As I was to realize later, he was the star of the department. The chairman, whom I first met on his return from summer vacation, was George Maughn. He was a large, tall man, a previous amateur heavy weight boxer, with huge hands. He was quite handsome, if somewhat fleshy, probably in his early fifties, at that time. He was considered by many as a rather forbidding man, who should not be trifled with. Despite his reputation, I can only say, that to me he was considerate, fair, generous and generally supportive. I am particularly grateful to him. At the end of my residency, even though I took the job in New York against his advice, he left the door open for me. At our good byes, he told me not to fret, if I do not like it there, as I would always be welcome back in his department. This generous offer gave me much confidence. Other members of the department also deserve some mention, among them a Dr. Philpott stood out. He was a very dynamic man, an experienced and a busy gynecologist who left an indelible impression. At that time, he was serving as president of the American College of O/G., which was quite a distinction, for a Canadian. He was also the previous chairman of the department. He gave founds for my co-resident and me, to travel to the States to attend an annual meeting of the American College of O/G in Atlantic City, which was at that time a

very dreary place, at the very end of it's former glory days. On the way there, Peter Beck, and I stopped in New York, where we managed to see "My Fair Lady", on the stage. There were several other professors who were very effective teachers, so overall, I felt that I received a good grounding in O/G. and I was very grateful to have had the opportunity to be trained at the Royal Victoria. The work however, was exhausting, often to the point numbness. We were required to be on call for thirty-six hours every second day. When on the evening off I was invited to a dinner, I would often leave in middle of conversation, to catch forty winks while sitting on the closed toilet. I would reappear refreshed, some time later. I would then pick up the conversation, where I left off, much to the confusion of my friends, as to what I was talking about or to where I have been.

Edith very quickly adjusted to her work at school, although she was given a very difficult task. The school principal, with the best intentions of finding Edith a position, created an additional class of ninth-graders. These students were selected from several other classes by their teachers who were obviously delighted to get rid of the worst troublemakers. Edith with her charm and persistence despite being mocked for her South African accent soon won them over and was very well accepted. Before Jillian was born, Edith was teaching to the very end, by which time her students overwhelmed her with gifts for her baby. She overheard some of the students, discussing what to give her at end of the school year for a present It resulted with the general agreement of "lets get her something for the kid". On the second of July 1959, Jillian was born. It was such a happy moment for us, yet at the same time we felt isolated, having no immediate family to share our joy. Jillian was mentally and physically a most advanced infant. At the age of six months she was able to sit. When she was given a soft toy resembling a dog for Christmas she managed to unwrap the parcel herself and uttered the sounds "wau wau." Edith's mother Meg, very kindly spent the first six months of Jiliian's life with us, which was of an enormous help in many ways.

Edith also, very quickly had quite a coterie of friends, both from among her fellow teachers, as well as, from some of our neighbors. I too, made some friends with my co-residents and their families. So overall, we felt accepted, if not yet exactly settled.

We very much treasured the hospitality of the van Beek family. Helen was a former high school mistress in England, while Karl was a local bank manager. He was a Canadian, with some family roots in South Africa. We were so lucky, to have been taken under their wing early on our arrival in Montreal. Although considerably older than we, they were very helpful and generous; even gave us some of their furniture, at the time when all we had was a mattress for a bed and a table made of boxes with a of sheet of plywood for a top. Helen and Karl was a very unusual couple for their age, at that time in Montreal. They were socially, and politically very liberal, were extremely well read and were truly some of the few intellectuals, which we had a privilege to count as friends.

The other family with whom we also remained friends for life was the Knafos. Ruby and David Knafo, could be best described as refugees from Morocco. They left because of the anti-Jewish hysteria, in response to the creation of the State of Israel. They were forced to leave their homeland, where their families lived for countless generations. Rubi was a well-educated woman, while David was an agronomist, who was in charge of large farms in Moroco. Ruby eventually became a celebrated teacher of French. In fact, she was charged with the responsibility of rewriting the entire French curriculum for the middle schools of the Province of Quebec. He on the other hand could find only a position with the Montreal Municipality, working in the parks department. He was soon to lose even this job, when he requested permission to be absent for the coming Jewish high holidays. Desperately seeking another employment, he opted to train as a hairdresser, eventually opening his own business. Sadly, both their lives ended in tragedy as Ruby died suddenly at the age of forty-eight, while David had become legally blind, following a complicated cataract operation. Edith deeply admired and loved Ruby. I still keep contact with David and his children. They all were, very dear friends.

While Edith soon felt at home in Montreal, I found it very much harder to acclimatize in the polarized atmosphere of the social, religious, cultural and the language divisions of this city. The French speaking Canadians, the majority of the population, were fiercely committed to their language and their Catholic faith. The Anglophones were predominantly Protestant and for most part of Scot descent. The other significant minority, were the Jews, who in large

measure was comprised of recent immigrants, first from Eastern Europe, then from Morocco. I found theses very sharp contrasts very uncomfortable. In the end so did later, many of the Anglophones of various ethnic and religious background. They left Quebec in large numbers, when the province threatened to separate from the rest of Canada. It also was then, when the provincial government instituted the French only policy, changing the longstanding bi-lingual character of the rest of Canada, which was in force since the establishment of the Dominion. This has lead eventually to a significant loss of commerce, for Quebec much to the economic detriment of its people. The cultural life was affected to a lesser degree because it was predominantly French oriented, anyway.

As time went by, despite the sharp linguistic, social or ethnic divisions of Montreal, we managed to lead quite a busy social life. There were the occasional concerts or recitals. I recall going to hear Ertha Kitt or Marlene Dietrich. Cinemas of course were common entertainment. Occasional balls or dances sponsored by the hospital were attended because of social obligations. Evening dinners with friends were common and welcome despite my chronic fatigue. The restaurants were generally very good; the lobsters were especially memorable, especially in the days before I developed a severe shellfish allergy. During the long and severe winter, we went skiing in the Laurentians, where we shared a cabin with friends. Despite the bitter cold and the rather short runs, it was real fun to be in the winter wonderland of the region. During the extremely cold temperatures, on occasions one virtually feared for ones health, if not for ones life.

At one time, Edith and I were truly lucky to escape almost certain death. We joined a group of friends to celebrate New Years Eve at a restaurant deep in the countryside of the Laurentian Mountains. By four a.m. I was tired and frankly bored, so decided to leave before the others. The restaurant was located in the edge of a frozen lake. The road leading from the main highway to the restaurant was a narrow lane, which was all iced up and rather uneven. On the way out instead turning right which would have taken me back on to the main road, I chose by mistake to go in the other direction. Very soon, we were out in the country without any signs of habitation. I falsely assumed that I was on a circular road, commonly encountered around the lakes, in the Laurentiens. After about two miles or so farther up, I

realized that we went the wrong way, when I found myself unexpectedly in a ditch at a dead end road and knee deep in snow. The only way out was to reverse straight up and to try to turn around on a flatter terrain. Needless to say, neither Edith nor I, were dressed warmly enough, to face prolonged exposure at 25 below if we tried to walk back. In desperation, with Edith in her high heel shoes and only a fur coat over a ball gown, pushing the front of the Volksvagen Beatle, we somehow managed to get out of the ditch in reverse. That was not the end of this misadventure however. On the way back while on the main high way, it was so cold that the accelerator froze to the floor of the car. Fortunately, there was very little traffic at that time. Only after we got home safely, we became overwhelmed by the reality of this near death experience.

The summers were also spent in the Laurentians, when I chose to spend my vacations as a camp doctor in a Boy Scout camp. Several times we had occasions to visit New York, for a long weekend, where we splurged on the theatre, seeing plays at the matinees and evening performances, both on the same day.

By the time my final year O/B residency finished, we had to decide where should we eventually settle. While Edith would very much have very much preferred to remain in Montreal, where she had good friends and established support systems but I could not practice there until I became a Canadian citizen. As this restriction did not apply to the Province of Ontario, I had no problem, getting a license there, having passed a national qualifying examination. We considered Toronto or its suburbs seriously as possible permanent places to live. It was the summer of 1959, when I was approached by Paul Latour, with a suggestion that I should look into position available in a newly established medical school in New York City. Apparently one of his colleagues, from the days as a pathology fellow at Harvard, just became, a chairman at the Albert Einstein College of Medicine and was recruiting a faculty. Dr. Latoure wrote a letter to Dr. Romney, which resulted in my being invited for an interview. I liked very much what I saw of the school, but I found my conversation with the chairman somewhat vague and disquieting. I decided not to accept a position there, which I planned to convey in letter. On my way out, I went to thank a senior member of the department, who very kindly took me around the institution. In the course of

our conversation, I clearly shared with him my negative impression and my reaction to the interview with the chairman. We entered in to long discussion and he persuaded me to reconsider. However, what really changed my mind was the sudden conviction, that both Edith and I might like very much living in New York. As I was walking the streets of Manhattan, on a beautiful sunny summer afternoon, sensing the vitality of the city, passing by the great stores, remembering how much we enjoyed the Broadway shows, I there and then my made up my mind to accept the job. For me it was a dramatic turn around for another reason, as we never seriously considered living in the USA. Now my only concern was to persuade Edith to accept the move to NY. On my return to Montreal, she responded to my enthusiasm and we began serious planning for the transition.

That was easier said than done. Getting to the States on the Polish visa allocation could take twenty years, so the only way to apply was on an essential workers' allocation. For this, one needed the support of an influential politician or a government official. Dr. Romney or the school fortunately managed to obtain such help from Senator Jacob Javits. By March of 1960 when we were granted a permanent visa, we were ready to move to New York. In the meantime, I had to undergo farther training in general surgery and internal medicine, so as to be eligible to sit for a specialty board examination in O/G by the Royal College of Surgeons of Canada. I spent the next eight months working at the Montreal Veterans Hospital. It was the least taxing period of my training. In preparation for my role as teacher and potential investigator, I sought permission to attend the weekly seminars conducted by Hans Salye at the Universite de Montreal. He was a very influential scientist, with worldwide recognition in Biology, for his very original contribution on the theory of stress. In fact he was the first person to write extensively on the effect of stress on health of animals and humans. Apparently, he was considered several times for the Nobel Prize. He was often a bride's maid but never a bride. I benefited much from this exposure to basic science, which I never had before.

IN THE LAND OF THE FREE AND THE HOME OF THE BRAVE

"New York New York is a Hell of a Town..."

or

If You Can Make It Here, You Can Make it Anywhere

I went by train to New York, lagging two huge suitcases, and then barely managed to get to the Bronx on the sub-way and eventually to Jacoby Hospital, where I was to work. I only stayed long enough to initiate the necessary employment formalities. I opened a bank account at the Chase Manhattan Bank to deposit enough money to buy a car. The following day I went to Larchmont where at the Hory Chevrolet I chose a two door white Impala. The same afternoon I left for Montreal, driving alone in my fancy new car through the night, in a mood of alternating excitement and anxiety. Once more and hopefully this time for good, I was to begin life in a new land alone, except for my nuclear family.

Now that I am nearing my 80th birthday, it is fitting that I should finally finish this memoir. I have been writing it on and off for six years and will conclude with an abstract of our life since we arrived in New York, late March of the year 1960. Edith Jillian as an eight- month old infant and I arrived on the campus of the Albert Einstein College of Medicine in the Bronx where we settled temporally in the students' residence. We were soon booted out, because my child's crying disturbed the students. In urgent need of housing we were recommended for an apartment on the Shore Road, in New Rochelle. All that was available at that time was a one bedroom flat and even this was difficult to find. It was however, near Glen Island with its park and the beach, which held a promise for a pleasant summer. These were hard times for my small family. We felt alone, without any support systems, devoid even of any friendly advice. We felt keenly all the pain of the newly arrived immigrants. My starting salary even for then was a paltry $7.500/year. Whatever savings we had, these were soon exhausted.

I started in the department of Obstetrics and Gynecology with the rank of an Instructor. The academic and the clinical department were then housed at the Jacobi General Hospital. I still

had to obtain the New York State license to practice Medicine, for which I had to write a Board examination. The campus of the College of the Albert Einstein Medical School in those days was a beehive of activity and enthusiasm, especially in the scientific research and student education. At that time, luckily for me, I came under the wing of Bob Davis, to whose laboratory I was directed by Dr. Romney the chair of O/G in an effort to learn some basics of scientific research. It was also there that I was exposed to a brilliant group of scientists investigating protein chemistry, headed by Paul Gallop. I had the privilege to sit at their seminars. The level of presentations were so complex that a co-author of a major textbook of Biochemistry Dr. Abe White who was also at that time the chairman of the department, when setting next to me one time, whispered, :I do not understand what they are talking about to which I retorted If you don't understand ,then I certainly don't belong here.

In the early days much I spent much of my in Bob's laboratory investigating micro-assays for createnine in dogs. Bob Davis was one of those few, who really deserved the appellation of a "Man for all Seasons". His medical, scientific and cultural attainments were extraordinary. He graduated from Harvard College and from the Medical School there. He then was awarded the prestigious two-year fellowship of the University, where he did research with Prof. Kostiakowski, who became the science adviser to President Eisenhower. Bob was most generous with his time and experience and I benefited much from his mentorship.

While I was working at the lab, I also had a large responsibility for student teaching. Once I obtained the license to practice medicine, I became progressively more involved in the patient care and the supervision of the residents. At that time, all we had for our clinical facilities was the Jacobi Hospital. I also gradually became involved with the care of the wives of the faculty and students, which I enjoyed very much. With time, I made many friends among them. This reminds of a vignette when many years later I was scrubbing for surgery at Montefiore Hospital, I was asked by a medical student if she could participate in the operation. As she was not on my service, I introduced myself, to which she retorted: Yes I know who you are, you delivered me. It was for me a sweet reward for the many sleepless nights I attended my colleagues' wives.

On February 10, 1961 our son, John, was born. Edith was delivered also at Jacobi without any undue difficulties. We were both jubilant and to celebrate at the bedside I bought a bottle of Chateaux I'Uquem, having asked for the best wine they had. I was truly not aware at that time, that this was, and still is, a wine of supreme quality. It proved to be a prescient symbol of the quality of man that John has become. It was also a time of additional stress for the us, having no family to help or to care. Here we were, rescued by the kind and generous help of Ruby Davis, Bob's wife. During Edith's hospitalization, she looked after Jillian in my absence and provided us daily with cooked meals for weeks afterwards. It was natural that we remained life-long friends with them and their children. Ned, their first born, became a distinguished scholar and a professor of Chinese history. John is a very talented performing pianist and musicologist and Elisabeth became a doctor, boarded both in Internal Medicine and Psychiatry with a recent appointment to the staff at the Massachusetts General Hospital. Ruby, not to be outdone by her distinguished family, is a respected interior designer of national stature.

After a period of relative hardships with help of friends, we bought a small house on Wayman Avenue in New Rochelle where we lived among a wonderful group of neighbors, most of whom were Italian-Americans. The other was the Kahn family. Helen Kahn was a sculptor of distinction and national recognition. We were fortunate to acquire one of her pieces called "The Bus Stop". At that time we also became quite friendly with two childless couples, the Wachtels and the Ziegners, who acted as substitute aunts and uncles to our children. "Aunt" Lou was for a long time very close to us, while through her husband Ed, an editor at Knopf, we met some interesting people.

We left this neighborhood with regret but managed to remain in touch for many years. We moved to Larchmont prompted by Jillian's need for a good middle school. It was one of those fortuitous decisions of a lifetime. When I had doubts as to the wisdom of buying our house, our dear friend Amy Cohen came through with a clincher, "George, you are buying a way of life, not a house." How wise she proved to be! Many years later I was able to provide similar advice to Bert Cohn, when he unexpectedly entered our living room with a

question if should he buy my neighbor Scheidlingers' house, to which I retorted: Don't buy grab it! I was well rewarded, as in Barbara and Bert, I was blessed with the sweetest neighbors and friends

Jillian and John entered their respective schools. They remained in the Mamaroneck-Larchmont school system until their graduation with grades good enough for admission to Amherst College. They graduated two years apart with Jillian going to the Duke University Medical School, while John attended a Master's program in Physics at Cornell University. Jillian remained at Duke, where she specialized in Psychiatry and John, after a year's teaching at a school in Brooklyn, did a Doctorate in English Literature at Stamford. Jillian having married Pablo Davanzo, left for Los Angeles where they both practiced psychiatry at UCLA. After twelve years there, they both moved into private practice; Jillian doing Adult, and Pablo, Child Psychiatry. They were blessed with a wonderful child, Zoe, who is a most beloved granddaughter and the sweetest, most generous and kind child, with artistic talents.

Living in Larchmont opened new vistas. We have made many new friends. The Katzenbergs introduced us to the Beachpoint Yacht Club and kindly included me in their tennis games. I am enormously grateful to Emily and Eugene Grant, whose hospitality and generosity is legendary and who have been so supportive, on occasions both happy and sad. What a wonderful experience it always was, to attend the children's concerts and various musical events sponsored and organized by Mitzi and Ted Cylkowski. They exposed our community, especially the children to the pleasures, discipline and the art of music. Mitzy became a lifelong friend , on whose wisdom and help, I thankfully rely. The Trumps, Stephanie, Jules and their children who are loving and kind and such pleasure to visit. There are so many others who have been such vital friends over the years who touched our lives, for which I shall be forever grateful.

John became a professor in the English department at Williams College in Williamstown, where he now lives with his brilliant wife Betsy Kolbert. She, after a very successful stint with the New York Times moved to the New Yorker Magazine, where she is a political correspondent. By now, they are both published authors, but their greatest achievement are

three wonderful sons. Ned, who was the first-born of our grandchildren, gave such joy to Edith, with whom he developed a very special bond. Mathew and Aaron have grown into bright, energetic and fine boys. It is a source of sorrow and regret for me, that Edith had so little time to share with me the joys and pleasure that our grandchildren give to me.

My own career proceeded gradually over the years, from an Instructor to a Professor Emeritus at Einstein, with a three years diversion as a Clinical Professor at the Yale University Medical School, while I was the Chairman of the Department at the Danbury Hospital. I am grateful for the opportunity for a professional life, which allowed me to function meaningfully in several areas. I was a clinician, teacher, investigator and administrator, all at the same time. I can truly say that I was never bored. Frustrated, annoyed, exhausted and on occasions, desperate, but bored never. Within an academic milieu of publish or perish, I had some fifty publications, many in peer reviewed journals, a book on "Suicide in Pregnancy" and a chapter in textbook of O/G. Some of my former students are physicians, now taking care of me. I made a decision for an academic career early in my professional life, so as to have time to see my children grow, at the expense of a larger income which a private practice might have provided. I am glad to say that I was very gratified by the outcome. An academic career also provided many opportunities for numerous national and overseas travels which often included the whole family. We had memorable trips in the U.S.A. We visited Europe, South Africa, Israel, Brasil, the Caribbean Islands and Mexico. On my sabbatical we took the children out of school for several months when they were still quite young to meet our families and friends in England and South Africa.

As I gather my thoughts to conclude this memoir, the memories of the past crowd my brain and fill my heart with great sadness that Edith died before she could fully enjoy the fruits of her incredible contributions to her family. Hers was a singular role in bringing up our children. She gave uncompromising love and attention with which she showered us all. Her extraordinary intellect, talents and energy will live with me forever. What luck I had to be brushed by this extraordinary human being, my life companion of fifty years.

Then when all seemed bleak and sad, unexpectedly life became worth living once again. Lorri and I had only tenuous contact with one another that of a personal trainer and a client. I continued with her services after Edith died, through the generosity and kindness of Amy Cohen. Lorri at that time was recently separated from her husband. Suddenly one day we realized that we were kindred souls. It seemed that our marked difference in ages did not really matter. I persuaded Lorri to move in me and we have been happy ever since. I found in Lorri a most wonderful, loving, funny, generous and kind companion. What luck at my age to find such happiness! I say without exaggeration that she brings me much joy. I am profoundly grateful to my children and my friends who opened their arms to us with love and understanding. I extend the same thanks to Lorri's family who treat me as their own. That I had the chance in one lifetime to have as companions such two wonderful human beings is a gift beyond hope.

EPILOGUE

I end my memoir the way I began, in stating my intention to describe some aspects of my life, which bears witness to the extraordinary injustice and a personal triumph of survival against impossible odds. Be mindful, that I remind the reader once more, that the credit is due in the end to a blind fate and not any "smarts". I have recently visited once again, the Holocaust Museum in Washington, where in the Hall of Remembrance, at the foot of the Altar with the Eternal flame, is this quote:

> *"ONLY GUARD YOURSELF AND GUARD YOUR SOUL*
>
> *CARFULLY, LEST YOU FORGET THE THINGS YOUR*
>
> *YOUR EYES SAW, AND LEST THESE THINGS DEPART*
>
> *YOUR HEART ALL THE DAYS OF YOUR LIFE. AND*
>
> *YOU SHALL MAKE THEM KNOWN TO YOUR*
>
> *CHILDREN AND YOUR CHILDREN'S CHILDREN.*
>
> Deuteronomy 4 : 9

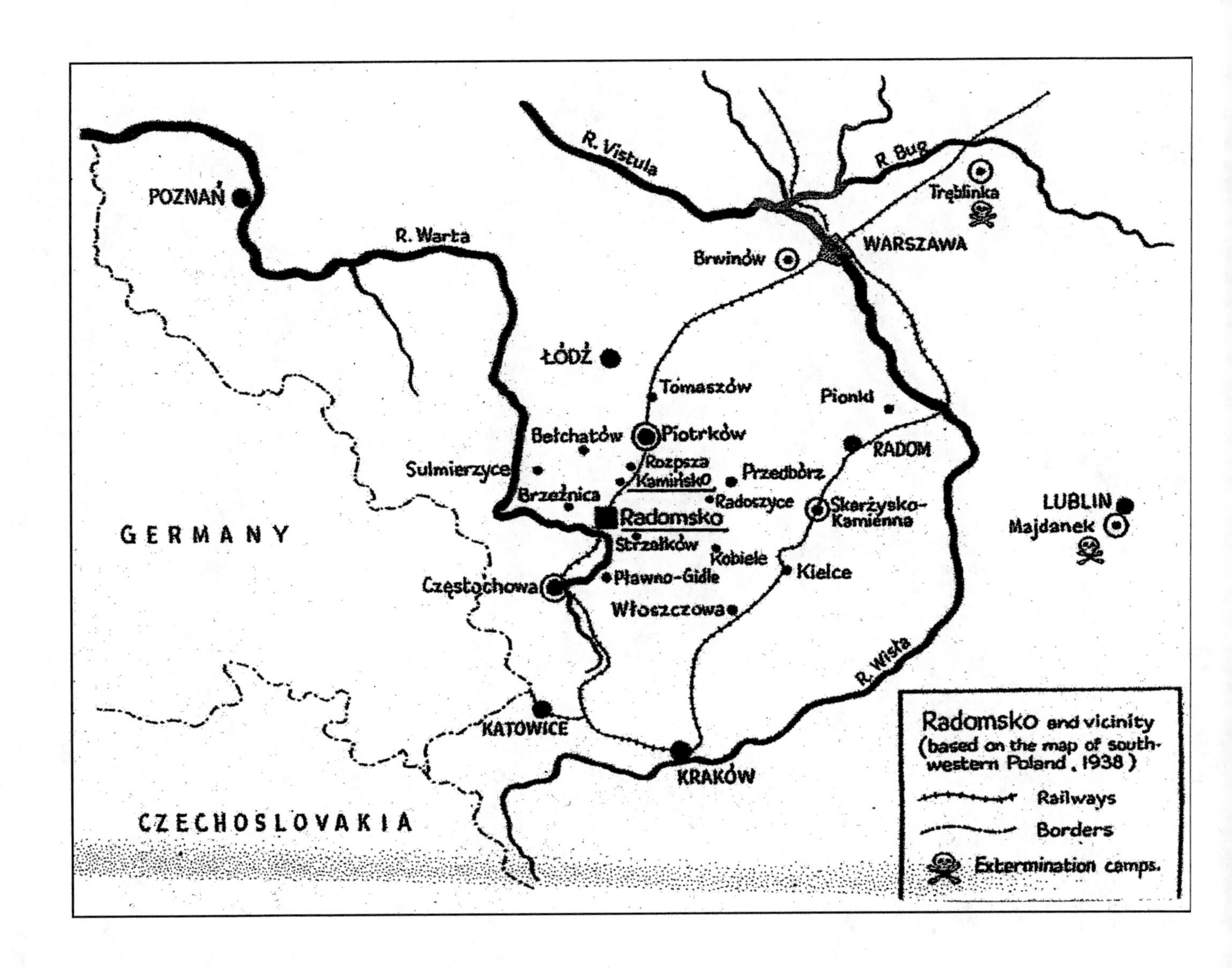
R. Vistula
R. Bug
Treblinka
POZNAŃ
R. Warta
Brwinów
WARSZAWA
ŁÓDŹ
Tomaszów
Pionki
Bełchatów
Piotrków
RADOM
Sulmierzyce
Rozpsza
Kamińsko
Przedbórz
Brzeźnica
Radoszyce
Skarżysko-Kamienna
LUBLIN
Majdanek
GERMANY
Radomsko
Strzałków
Kobiele
Kielce
Częstochowa
Pławno-Gidle
Włoszczowa
R. Wisła
KATOWICE
KRAKÓW
CZECHOSLOVAKIA
Radomsko and vicinity
(based on the map of south-western Poland, 1938)
Railways
Borders
Extermination camps.

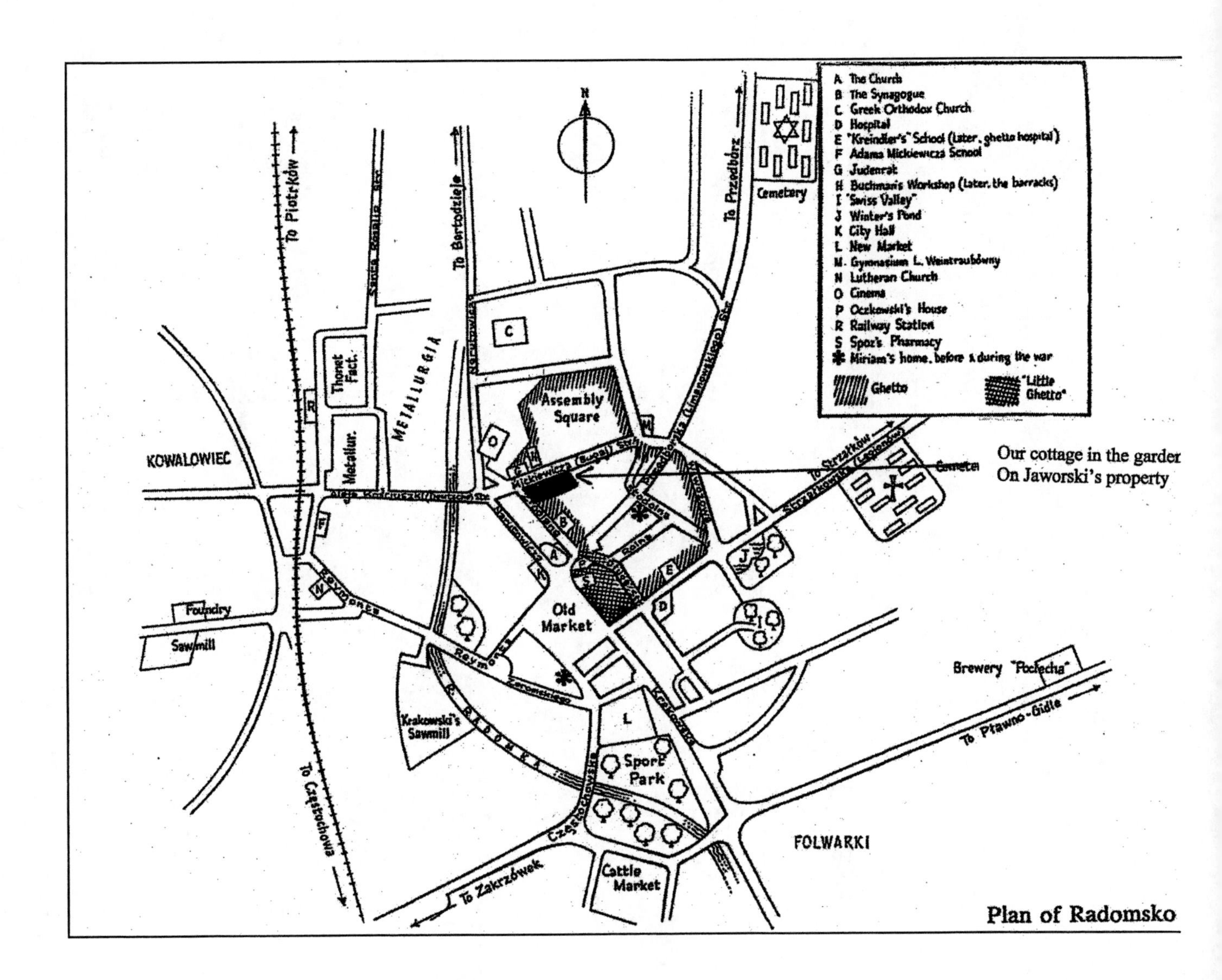

Plan of Radomsko

Ludwik and classmates at matriculation time

Mother and Father at the Spa

My Parents, Bella, our maid, and I.
Note the barn in the background

My Parents and friends rafting on the River Porad. I did a similar trip.

Bronka Novak and I, the Ghetto wall in the background.

FRAGMENTS OF ONE OF HAPPIEST MORNINIG OF MY LIFE

The first time I met my brother Bob after the war,a hiatus of six years.
It was such an endless time of waiting and doubt if this day would ever come.

After a sleepless night of cavorting

Gathering gooseberries

Helga,Bob,Zosia,Margareta,Jan & I.

On the boulevards with friends

With Bob's friends

In the Louvre with M.L.

In the British Officers' Casino

The sailor who helped

Ludwik in England

Bob ,his navigator and a friend

First day in uniform

Ludwik an I in London

Audrey, I and a friend at Regents Park

Audrey, Ms.Lee and I

Mr.Posey and I
In
Burchington

On the way to South Africa

Canary Islands

Me, at the helm???

Marisia Rosenberg, her son George,
I and some friends.
Johannnesburg, the early days.

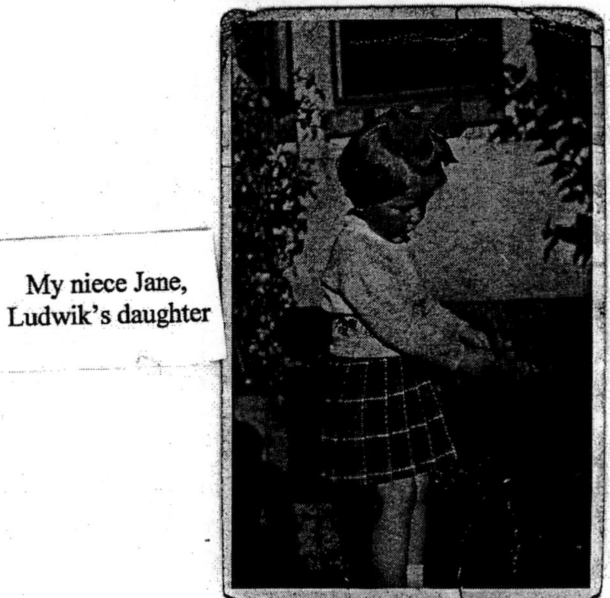

My niece Jane,
Ludwik's daughter

Bob's Children, my nephews
Robert,James,Peter and niece
Barbara ,in Johannesburg '57

The memorial to the martyred Jews of Radomsko
At the infamous extermination camp of Treblinka.